Yuen Kay-San

WING CHUN KUEN

History and Foundation

Rene Ritchie

阮奇山詠春拳

Multi-Media Books · Los Angeles and New York

DISCLAIMER

Please note that the author and publisher of this book are NOT RESPONSIBLE in any manner whatsoever for any injury that may result from practicing the techniques and/or following the instructions given within. Since the physical activities described herein may be too strenuous in nature for some readers to engage in safely, it is essential that a physician be consulted prior to training.

First published in 1998 by Multi-Media Books,
a division of Multi-Media Communications Network, Inc.

Copyright © 1997 by Rene Ritchie

Library of Congress Cataloging Card Number: 98-68040

ISBN: 1-892515-03-2

Distributed by
Unique Publications
4201 Vanowen Place
Burbank, CA 91505
(800) 332–3330

First edition
05 04 03 02 01 00 99 98 97 1 3 5 7 9 10 8 6 4 2
Printed in the United States of America

Designed by Gilbert Cheah   •   Edited by Mark V. Wiley

Table of Contents

教
石
奇

I first began my studies of wing chun kuen in the mid-1960s, during the turbulent times of the Cultural Revolution. I consider myself fortunate to have had the opportunity to study under grandmaster Sum Nung, the disciple of Yuen Kay-San, and would like to express my heartfelt gratitude to him for all he taught me over the years. With deep insight into the concepts of the art and profound experience in its application, he is both a great teacher and gifted martial artist.

As a martial art, wing chun kuen is intelligent, calm, and practical. I also found it to be a great way to stay healthy. I very much enjoyed my time spent learning wing chun kuen and although it was in the best interests of my family, I regretted leaving my teacher and classmates behind when I moved to Canada in 1982. I believe that had I remained in Guangzhou, I would still be showing up for practice to this day.

When I arrived in Canada, I did not know the language and had to work very hard to support my family. Long ago, my teacher told me that wing chun kuen could be like a winter jacket—you could put in the closet for a time when you were unable to use it, but could always pull it out again when needed. Thus, while family commitments forced me to put my wing chun kuen away for many years, when the opportunity presented itself in 1990 I took on a small group of students and began passing on what I remembered.

Grandmaster Sum Nung also told me that Yuen Kay-San wing chun kuen concepts should be preserved and could be a powerful tool for making friends. Over the years, I have found this to be true and several of my students have turned out to not only be dedicated practitioners, but great friends as well.

From the beginning, some of my students, such as Rene Ritchie, showed an interest in the details of the art and so I encouraged them to take notes and come to me with any questions they might have. Rene also developed an interest in the history of wing chun kuen and managed to locate many old articles and other materials on the system. It was my pleasure to help him translate many of these articles, an activity that helped improve my knowledge of English and started him on the road to learning the Chinese language.

At first, I was surprised at how much information on the Yuen Kay-San system had already made it into print. The Yuen Kay-San system had always been rather closely held, yet Rene found articles detailing many of the concepts and principles, as well as full demonstrations of versions of the "kidney breathing return invigoration," "wooden dummy methods," and other elements. He also showed me tapes of public demonstrations involving much of the style. Although a lot of this material was very good, it was spread out over many different works and much of it was unavailable or indecipherable to people in the West. This meant that while wing chun kuen in general was well known, the contributions of Yuen Kay-San and grandmaster Sum Nung remained almost unheard of outside China and its surrounding areas.

In addition, it seemed some of the Yuen Kay-San material had also found its way, perhaps accidentally, into the publications of other wing chun branches. Lastly, in some cases information on Yuen Kay-San had at times been presented to the public that was at odds with what grandmaster Sum Nung had passed along within the system.

It was with all of the above in mind that Rene went forward with this book. It follows on the heels of his brief introductions of the art both in print and on the Internet, and his co-authoring of the book Complete Wing Chun.

I am very happy that Rene has written this book and given an insight into grandmaster Sum Nung's art to the Western public. I am also very pleased that my students Antony Casella and Georgia Dow were able to help so much with its successful completion.

In closing, I would like to point out that despite my improvements in English and the efforts my students have made to understand Cantonese, it remains very difficult to accurately record the system in print, especially in another language. Thus, I hope readers will forgive any errors or omissions that may have crept into this book or its transmission.

I firmly believe that the legacy of Yuen Kay-San and the teachings of grandmaster Sum Nung are among the priceless treasures of the martial arts world. I hope others find their insights as valuable as I have.

朱
壽
禮

It was my pleasure to be given the honor of writing the forward to this excellent book. I came to know about Rene Ritchie a while back when I read his article *Yuen Kay-San Wing Chun Kuen* in the May 1995 issue of Martial Art Masters magazine. I was very impressed with his style of writing; it was very informative and concise. It was also very close to the source of Yuen Kay-San wing chun kuen through Ngo Lui-Kay sifu, who studied with the gatekeeper of the art, grandmaster Sum Nung.

I started training in Yuen Kay-San wing chun kuen in 1981 under the tutelage of Kwan Jong-Yuen, my Yuen Kay-San and Gulao wing chun kuen instructor. At that time, I had already been learning and practicing the Yip Man branch of wing chun kuen for over seven years. Learning the Yuen Kay-San system was different for me. Coming straight from China, it seemed to have elements not taught in the Yip Man system, including the 12 keywords, 12 basic san sao of Cheung Bo, *sun hei gwai yuen hei gung*—a form of internal training to invigorate the kidneys—and a unique wooden dummy set. Over the years, articles and visitors from Mainland China have enriched my knowledge of the Yuen Kay-San wing chun kuen family.

In 1988 I moved from New York to Los Angeles. Having learned and experienced the Yip Man, Yuen Kay-San, and Gulao systems, I continued to do research on other wing chun kuen branches. Later that year, I wrote an article for the Spring 1990 issue of the *Wing Chun Kuen Viewpoint* newsletter, which I believe was the first overview of the Yuen Kay-San system published in North America—although perhaps in limited distribution.

Several years passed before I saw Rene's article in Martial Arts Masters magazine. Coincidentally, I had also just begun to surf the Internet at that time. It was there that I came across the *Yuen Kay-San Homepage*, written and hosted by Rene. Upon a quick review, I wrote to Rene and we struck up an immediate rapport as a result of our common interest—Yuen Kay-San wing chun kuen. We wrote daily, sometimes several times a day, regarding practice, experience, and problems studying wing chun kuen. Unlike many practitioners of the art I have met, Rene was very open minded to the various branches and practices of wing chun kuen and other martial arts out there.

During the next year, Rene and another gentleman he met on the Internet, Y. Wu of Singapore, came up with the idea of writing a book on the history and traditions of wing chun kuen and enlisted my help. For over two years, the three of us corresponded almost daily on this task, gathering bits of data on the various branches of wing chun kuen and their historical traditions. We had to sort through all of the nonsense, self-appreciating propaganda, and the desire of some individuals to self-promote through fairy tales. We shared our information with the wing chun kuen community as we came out with it through the webpages Rene set up and maintained. These included the *Yuen Kay-San Wing Chun Kuen Homepage, Wing Chun Kuen Archives, Chu Sau Lei Wing Chun Kuen Homepage, Gulao Wing Chun Kuen Homepage, Chi Sim Ving Tsun Homepage,* and more (information on these can be retrieved at http://www.wingchunkuen.com). The finished book was published in the summer of 1988 by the Charles E. Tuttle Co. under the title *Complete Wing Chun: The Definitive Guide to the History and Traditions of Wing Chun Kung-Fu.* Our research made it possible to link all the branches of the wing chun kuen family and provide a consistent glossary of terms and concepts used in the various wing chun kuen systems. We were proud and happy to share this labor of love with the wing chun kuen community.

With that project over, Rene decided to focus his energy on his teacher's art, and this excellent book is the result. *Yuen Kay-San Wing Chun Kuen* is the crowning achievement of this young sifu's talents. I am sure that Rene will go on to even greater achievements and it is with my highest recommendations that those interested in wing chun kuen or martial arts in general read this book.

I was fortunate to learn the Yuen Kay-San wing chun kuen system from Ngo Lui-Kay (Ao Leiqi), a student of grandmaster Sum Nung. Although Ngo was born in Hong Kong in 1934, he moved to the Mainland in the early 1950s to study at a university outside Beijing. After graduation he traveled Northern China and Korea with the army before settling down in the city of Guangzhou. Since his youth he had had a desire to study the martial arts, yet had been unable to find that which he sought—a great style, and a great teacher. In Guangzhou, however, Ngo Lui-Kay heard of wing chun kuen and was drawn to it by its practicality and usefulness. He was then fortunate to find an extraordinary teacher of the art in grandmaster Sum Nung. The combination of an intelligent system that was refined and yet effective and a teacher who understood and could explain the system in its most minute of details was more then Ngo Lui-Kay could have hoped for. He began training under grandmaster Sum Nung in the mid-1960s and followed him for approximately a decade and a half. Working hard and practicing regularly, Ngo devoted himself to the development of his wing chun kuen skills.

In 1982, with the help of his uncle, Ngo Lui-Kay was able to move his family to Canada. For a long time in Canada, Ngo Lui-Kay kept his knowledge of wing chun kuen quiet and accepted no students, preferring to invest his time in his business, working hard and trying to secure a future for his family.

I first encountered wing chun kuen and the Yuen Kay-San system in 1990 when I met Ngo Lui-Kay. At the time, I was practicing other martial arts. Ngo sifu, however, took the time to speak with Antony Casella and me. He demonstrated the "inside joining" technique, pointing out that with his positioning, one of my arms was fully controlled while the other was out of range. In essence, both of his fists could touch me easily, while neither of mine could get near him. Impressed with both his generous nature and ingenious system, we asked Ngo sifu for instruction. On two occasions, assisted by the translations of his daughter, Ngo sifu introduced us, as well as Georgia Dow and a small group of others, to Yuen Kay-San wing chun kuen. The introduction consisted of the meridian punch, the side punch, the single dragon punch, and the arrow punch along with a demonstration of the siu lien tao form. I remember being mesmerized by the snake-like movements of his cross-shaped hand and stunned at the flexible power he generated over the shortest of distances.

I did not see Ngo sifu for several months after that. I did, however, discover that his daughter was attending the same college as myself. Whenever I bumped into her, I would always inquire about her father and eventually a few others and I called and arranged to continue our instruction. We started again at the beginning, working on basic horses and punching for the first few months. Over those months, a few people stopped attending and a few others began (some joining us again from those two early classes). Of those who remained more than a short time, myself, Antony Casella, Georgia Dow, David Johnson, and Deon Weir formally began learning during this period. A few students our teacher had recently taken in Chinatown, including Wilson Woo also joined us during the first few weeks.

In honor of and with respect for his ancestors, Ngo Lui-Kay was determined to share his knowledge and to help preserve the art of Yuen Kay-San and the teachings of grandmaster Sum Nung.

It is in order to help preserve the art that Ngo sifu supported and encouraged me in the writing of this book. It is our firm belief that grandmaster Sum Nung's Yuen Kay-San system is an exceptional form of martial arts and our sincerest hope that fellow practitioners, newcomers, and interested readers alike find this volume beneficial.

I would like to express heartfelt thanks first and foremost to my sifu, Ngo Lui-Kay, for sharing with me grandmaster Sum Nung's teachings of Yuen Kay-San's art and for his continual encouragement and assistance with this project and many others. Thanks as well for the use of his historical photographs and for his patience and generosity in posing for the forms presented in this volume. It is hard to find a good teacher, harder to find a good teacher who will teach you properly, and hardest of all to find such a teacher who is also a good person and great friend. My classmates and I were blessed to find such a teacher in Ngo Lui-Kay sifu.

I would also like to thank my classmates Antony Casella, Georgia Dow, David Johnson, Deon Weir, Wilson Woo, and all the rest. Special thanks to Antony Casella and Georgia Dow for their help with the photographs and text.

Thanks to Y. C. Yeung for his accounts from grandmaster Sum Nung and Yuen Jo-Tong; to Teddy Wong sifu for sharing his accounts of the art and Michael Engle for his hospitality; to Dan Lam, Bud Shapard, Ben Eller, and the rest of the Yuen Kay-San family with whom I have had the good fortune of discussing the art. Although too many to name here, each has helped me form a well-rounded and encompassing view of the system.

I also would like to thank Roger D. Hagood and *Martial Arts of China* magazine for the use of the photo of Lee Chi-Yiu sifu; Y. Wu, one of my co-authors on *Complete Wing Chun*; Jim Roselando, and the many other wing chun kuen enthusiasts I have had a chance to converse with over the years. And to the Internet wing chun Kuen Mailing List, created and maintained by Marty Goldberg and Robert Gillespie, an outstanding forum for exchange among wing chun kuen practitioners (information on the WCML can be obtained at http://www.wingchunkuen.com/wcm).

Thanks to Mark V. Wiley, author of *Filipino Martial Arts: Cabales Serrada Escrima* and *Filipino Martial Culture*, publishing manager of Multi-Media Books and editor of *Martial Arts Illustrated* magazine. My editor on *Complete Wing Chun* and this volume, Mark brings to our projects enthusiasm and expertise in not only publishing but in the martial arts as well.

Special thanks go to Robert Chu (Chu Sau-Lei), student of Kwan Jong-Yuen and descendant of Kwok Jin-Fen's branch of grandmaster Sum Nung's teachings. My co-author on *Complete Wing Chun* and a true martial arts brother, Robert began his journey down wing chun kuen's path long before I and has been generous enough to share his thoughts with me along the way. Our conversations have greatly enriched my knowledge and widened my understanding of the many versions of wing chun kuen and the martial arts in general.

Lastly, but certainly not least, I give thanks to my family for their support in this and everything else over the years.

The martial arts of China, known as *mo sut* (*wu shu*) or *kuen faat* (*quan fa*, boxing methods) and colloquially referred to as *kung fu* (*gong fu*, skill attained through hard work over time), are many and varied. Recent surveys have estimated that hundreds of distinct styles, and perhaps thousands of sub-styles and variant branches have developed within China's borders.

Chinese martial arts are typically divided into *bak kuen* (*bei quan*, northern boxing)—styles originating north of the Changjian (Yangtze) River—and *nam kuen* (*nan quan*, southern boxing)—styles originating south of the river. It is in the latter category, along with such famed arts as Hung ga kuen (Hung family boxing) and Choy Lee Fut (Choy, Lee, and Buddha boxing), that wing chun kuen belongs. In this sense, it is often grouped alongside arts like bak hok kuen (white crane boxing) and sae ying kuen (snake form boxing), and related systems such as nam tong long kuen (southern mantis boxing), bak mei kuen (white eyebrow boxing), lung ying mo kiu (dragon form rubbing bridges), and others.

Some also attempt to classify the martial arts into *ngoi ga* (*waijia*, external/outside family) and *noi ga* (*neijia*, internal/inside family). These are indistinct terms, however, and have varied considerably in interpretation over the years. Originally, the terms may have been used to separate Buddhist teaching and exercises, which originated outside of China from Taoist ones, which originate inside China. In the simplest sense, however, and perhaps the only sense of the terms used in southern boxing, wing chun kuen was kept very much "inside the family" (not taught to outsiders) until the 1950s. In terms of "internal" and "external," "soft" and "hard," wing chun kuen (like most refined arts) defies labels. It favors instead the meridian (center) line approach. Embracing a balanced method it flows freely between both while being firmly bound to neither.

Wing chun kuen's labeling as "classical" and "modern" is also at times a source of confusion. Wing chun kuen is ancient in that it is built upon a solid foundation of thousands of years of Chinese martial development, encompassing the traditional core of the classical arts. It is recent in that it has continued this development into the present day, firmly embracing modern, scientific principles and highly refined concepts. As a result, when people come to understand wing chun kuen they can look at any Chinese martial art and see the same core. This may be why, over the years, so many different arts have been linked to wing chun kuen's origin.

Lastly, wing chun kuen has the rather strange distinction of being at the same time one of the most widely recognized and often practiced martial arts of China and an art of many unique branches about which many people are completely unaware.

The Yuen Kay-San system of wing chun kuen is one of these rare and elusive branches.

Part of the reason for the lack of information on many of the wing chun kuen branches was the traditional veils of secrecy that sought to obscure the art and the anti-Manchurian revolutionary movement that surrounded it. Yuen Kay-San himself continued this tradition in his own way. An intensely private man, Yuen did much to discourage the publicity of his art. In spite of his wishes, however, Yuen's skills were such that he still gained a great reputation for his wing chun kuen in early 20th century Foshan, Guangdong. By the 1920s and '30s, local authors such as Au Soi-Jee had begun to record his exploits in the newspapers and in books such as *Six-and-a-Half-Point Pole*.

The rise of the People's Republic of China was another great factor in keeping the style in relative obscurity. Yuen Kay-San passed away just a few short years after the Communists took power and the conditions facing his successor, grandmaster Sum Nung, were far less hospitable then those faced in Hong Kong and other outside areas. During the Cultural Revolution and the years surrounding it, the practice of martial arts was discouraged, sometimes violently, at times even fatally. Thus, many of China's ancestral fighting arts were driven underground. Some arts became almost extinct in their own lands of origin while others were later reformed into modern sport wushu. Wing chun kuen was fortunate in that its small frame was ideal for practice in even confined areas. The art could thus be trained quietly behind closed doors.

Not wanting to attract attention, grandmaster Sum Nung preserved his art privately, teaching only small groups of trusted students. While his reputation grew in Guangdong, outside the Bamboo Curtain his art remained mysterious. This began to slowly change in the late 1960s when some of his students moved outside China. Yuen Kay-San's art also eventually resurfaced in the media. Leung Dai-Chiu, Kwok Wan-Ping, and Lee Chi-Yiu all contributed to articles on the Yuen Kay-San system, its history and its methods, in Hong Kong. Their efforts, for the first time, made real information on Yuen Kay-San wing chun kuen available to the outside world, albeit the Chinese reading world. One of the most prolific writers on behalf of the Yuen Kay-San system is Yuen's grandson, Jo-Tong. Yuen Jo-Tong has written articles on both Yuen Kay-San and grandmaster Sum Nung. These articles have helped to correct much of the misinformation that continued to circulate about the system despite the efforts of grandmaster Sum Nung's students.

To Western enthusiasts—especially those without access to Chinese magazines or knowledge of written Chinese—the art remained almost unheard of. Aside from a short interview and video sequence made available by Thomas Wong and introductory articles by Robert Chu and Rene Ritchie, it was not until the publication of *Complete Wing Chun* that information on the Yuen Kay-San branch became readily available to the general public.

Following on the heels of *Complete Wing Chun*, this volume hopes, for the first time, to share the fundamentals of the Yuen Kay-San system with enthusiasts around the world.

Notes on Variations

Yuen Kay-San wing chun kuen is not a singular phenomenon. Over the years grandmaster Sum Nung has taught many, many outstanding students, each with their own individual insights and personal tastes. Thus, while all from the same source, each has preserved his/her own unique interpretation of the art. As this book could not hope to properly document them all, it will attempt to document what the author has learned from Ngo Lui-Kay sifu. Other interpretations may vary.

Notes on Language

Yuen Kay-San wing chun kuen began its modern development in the city of Foshan, Guangdong and continued on in the nearby provincial capitol of Guangzhou. Guangdonghua (Cantonese) is thus the mother tongue of the art, and the language and dialect in which we will present the personal, conceptual, and technical names in this book. Since most modern maps render the names of places in the official People's Republic of China dialect and romanization, Mandarin *pinyin*, we will maintain that convention herein.

While Mandarin enjoys the increasingly popular *pinyin* method of romanization, no such standard has yet been accepted for the romanization of Guangdonghua. Thus, since wing chun kuen first began to be transmitted to English speaking students, many different methods have evolved to "spell" the words using the Roman alphabet. To simplify things for this book, we have explored many of the different popular romanizations, and chosen those we felt best rendered the sounds involved.

PART ONE

源流

Origins

CHAPTER 1

Legends of Wing Chun Kuen

Many of the famed martial arts of southern China were founded during the Ching (Manchurian) dynasty by revolutionaries. To them, secrecy could mean the difference between surviving to continue the fight and execution at the hands of the Manchurians. Thus, to protect themselves and their cause, they passed along inspiring fables that covered their activities, hid their true identities, and stirred the hearts of the people. Over the generations, these stories have become an inextricable part of Chinese martial culture and given rise to the many and varied legends associated with the southern Chinese martial arts.

The folk stories of wing chun kuen are some of the best known and often heard. So common are they, in fact, that many have forgotten their origins and assumed them to be factual accounts. In truth, while they may contain some historic elements and do much to enhance the mystique, romance, and rich texture of the style, they should never be mistaken for history.

It should also be noted that many major and minor variations exist for these stories. Presented below are a selection of some of the more commonly told wing chun kuen legends in China.

Ng Mui

Legends hold that the art that would become wing chun kuen began roughly 200 years ago with the nun Lui Sei-Leung, who was known by the Buddhist name Ng Mui (Five Plums). An ardent supporter of the rebellions, Ng Mui fled the destruction of the Young Forest (Shaolin) Temple in Fujian province and, hunted by Ching troops, sought refuge at the White Crane Temple nestled high atop the Emei Mountains in Sichuan province. One day, her meditation was disturbed by violent sounds coming from the nearby brush. Upon investigation, Ng Mui was startled to find two animals—a snake and a crane—locked in mortal combat.

The snake was calm and supple yet struck with incredible swiftness. The crane was patient and would wait until the last second before countering with deadly precision. Ng Mui was entranced with what she saw and began studying the animals intensely. Using her own martial arts knowledge as a foundation, she was soon coiling and darting like the snake and angling and intercepting like the crane. Their movement inspired her movement; her arms and hands like the body and fangs of the serpent and wings and claws of the bird. Not merely imitating the creatures, Ng Mui came to understand the concepts behind their actions and adapted them to suit her own human nature. Melding her new insights with her previous knowledge, she found they complemented each other perfectly. Since the noble crane had ultimately proven victorious in the encounter, Ng Mui named her new art "white crane boxing" in its honor.

Miu Shun

苗
順

Ng Mui eventually left the temple and journeyed south through Yunnan and east into Guangxi province. There she encountered a monk by the name of Miu Shun. Impressed with his character and sensing great talent in him, Ng Mui decided to teach him her white crane boxing. Miu Shun, intelligent and already possessing a strong martial arts foundation, proved to be a quick study and an excellent pupil.

When Ng Mui left to resume her travels, Miu Shun continued to polish his skills. Combining the nun's white crane boxing with his previous martial knowledge and refining both, he developed a new, as yet unnamed art.

Yim Yee

嚴
二

Yim Yee, also known as Yim Sei, first learned martial arts in his native Fujian province at the Young Forest Temple. In Fujian Yim had been a part of the rebellious Red Sect's militant Red Pole division. It was the goal of the sect to "overthrow the Ching and return the Ming" to the throne of China. To this end they plotted assassinations and other acts of revolt. When the Manchurians discovered their plans, however, Yim Yee fled to escape arrest and certain execution.

Settling with his infant daughter in Guangxi, Yim Yee established a small tofu shop and came to be known by the locals as Grandfather Yee. Meeting Miu Shun, he also became the monk's sole disciple and learned the blended art of Ng Mui.

Yim Wing-Chun

嚴
詠
春

Yim Yee's daughter was named Yim Wing-Chun and was also known by the name Yim Sum-Leung. At a very young age she began learning martial arts from her father. By day they would sell tofu in their shop; by night they would train their fighting skills. Through hard work and dedication, Wing-Chun managed to build a strong foundation. Bright and insightful, she soon realized, however, that she neither possessed the size nor strength of the typical martial artist. Thus, when learning from her father, Wing-Chun adapted the art to suit her own nature and build.

Leung Bok-Lao

梁
博
鎏

Leung Bok-Lao was a Jiangxi native and another former revolutionary and Young Forest Temple student who had fled to Guangxi. One of his favorite foods being tofu, he dropped by the Yee family shop soon after arriving in town and was surprised by the unsurpassed quality of their product.

One night, while walking outside, he chanced to see Yim Wing-Chun practicing her martial arts beneath the moonlight. He instantly fell in love with her beauty, grace, and skill. Hoping to learn the martial art he had seen, and taken with the young lady Yim, Leung Bok-Lao asked Grandfather Yee for a job and place to stay. Discovering they had similar backgrounds, Yim Yee agreed.

Realizing that he was growing older, and seeing that while as yet unspoken, the feelings between Wing-Chun and Bok-Lao ran deep, Yim Yee arranged for them to be married.

When Yim Yee passed away soon thereafter, Yim Wing-Chun and Leung Bok-Chao decided to close the tofu shop and move on. They traveled around for a while and eventually settled in Zhaoqing, Guangdong.

During this time, Leung Bok-Lao wished to further study the methods of his wife, but lacked the patience to do so in a step-by-step manner. Wing-Chun pointed out that with his combined knowledge of Young Forest boxing and her father's methods, Bok-Lao already knew more techniques then she and had to look beyond the raw material. Finally, in an effort to help her husband gain understanding, Wing-Chun offered to have a friendly match with him. Although initially hesitant, Bok-Lao eventually agreed only to discover quickly that his skills were no match for those of his wife. His lesson learned, he followed her advice and spent as much time as possible practicing her methods.

A short time later Yim Wing-Chun became sick and passed away. In loving memory of his wife, Leung Bok-Lao called his martial art "Wing-Chun's boxing," so that her name and legacy would live on.

The Red Junk Opera

At that time in Foshan there was a Red Junk Opera Company named Red Flower Union. Among the more famous members were Wong Wah-Bo, Leung Yee-Tai, Painted Face Kam, and Tall Man Chung. The opera would often travel the route between Zhaoqing and Guangzhou, and one day Leung Bok-Lao decided to attend the performance. Their technique was superb and Leung Bok-Lao was very impressed. Wanting to make friends with the performers, he arranged an introduction.

Leung Bok-Lao and the opera performers became fast friends and he was shocked to discover that they too practiced an art with the almost identical sounding name of "Weng Chun boxing," this one meaning "Always Spring" and descending from Young Forest Temple abbot Jee Shim.

Jee Shim

When Leung Bok-Lao inquired about the origins of Always Spring boxing, the actors related that one day, a mysterious beggar had approached their boat and demanded passage to Guangzhou. When Leung Yee-Tai had refused the man, the beggar had come over and placed one foot on the deck of the boat, planting the other firmly on the dock. He then assumed a deep horse and defied the young poler to move the boat. Laughing at first, Leung pushed off with his staff, thinking he could easily displace the beggar and teach him a lesson with an impromptu bath. The poler was startled, however, when he was unable to move the boat so much as an inch.

Performer Painted Face Kam soon roused Wong Wah-Bo, the most physically powerful member of their troupe, and asked him to help out. In number, the opera members again tried to push the boat out of the dock. None could believe it when even their combined effort failed completely. Recognizing that the beggar was obviously more then he seemed, Wong Wah-Bo and company approached him and bowing, offered him passage.

During the voyage to Guangzhou, the beggar revealed himself as Jee Shim, abbot in hiding of the Fujian Young Forest Temple. Thinking that the opera performers could be valuable members of the rebellion, he offered to teach them his martial arts. Jee Shim had previously taught the fighting arts in the Young Forest Temple's Always Spring Hall. Desiring to hide the Young Forest name from the Ching troupes who still hunted for it, the Red Junk troupe called their art Always Spring boxing after the hall. (The opera performers became particularly skilled in Jee Shim's famed six-and-a-half-point long pole.) Leung Bok-Lao, like Jee Shim before him, felt they would make exceptional students to help preserve his wife's art. Deciding to teach them, he traveled with the Red Junk performers for a time, before leaving for the north.

The Red Junk actors thus became proficient in not only the Young Forest "Always Spring boxing" of Jee Shim, but the Ng Mui derived "Praise Spring boxing" of Yim Wing-Chun as well. Using Leung Bok-Lao's teachings, they refined Jee Shim's methods and long pole and added them to the system. When they retired, they each took on their own students and the wing chun kuen art began to spread into Foshan and surrounding areas.

CHAPTER 2

History of Wing Chun Kuen

The roots of what would one day become wing chun kuen began with the anti-Ching revolutionary movements that arose in response to the Manchurian invasion of China in 1644. Groups such as the Tien Dei Wui (Heaven and Earth Society) and Hung Moon (Red Sect), organized with the goal of *fan ching fook ming* (overthrowing the Ching dynasty and returning the Ming). Many highly skilled and innovative martial artists were involved with the revolutionary movements, including the ancestors of wing chun kuen.

The name wing chun kuen is derived from these times. The term *wing* means "words issuing perpetually from the mouth—to chant, praise, or sing" while *chun* refers to "the sun causing plants to burst forth—the spring" and *kuen* to "the hand rolled up—fist or boxing." In revolutionary terms, this meant that no matter how bad the winter (Ching rule) the Han people should always praise (work with determination towards) the spring (re-blossoming of the Ming dynasty), utilizing in part this system of boxing.

The secrecy necessitated by the times has led, over the generations, to much confusion and made it almost impossible to distill the true origins of wing chun kuen from amid all the cover stories. The first period to which the history of wing chun kuen can even begin to be reliably traced is that of the Red Junk Opera Company of the mid-19th century.

The Red Junk Opera

紅
船
戲
班

The Hung Suen Hei Ban (Red Junk Opera Company) was a group of performers who traveled throughout Guangdong province entertaining the locals with their famed blend of song, acrobatics, and martial arts. The Red Junks derived their name from the heavily decorated boats the performers used to travel up and down the rivers between cities such as Zhaoqing, Foshan, and Guangzhou.

Since the performers could move around with relative ease, wore heavy make-up and elaborate costumes that could disguise their appearances, and often used fictitious stage names and nicknames that could cover their identities, the opera company was an ideal hiding place for revolutionaries.

紅
花
會
館

The Red Flower Union

Histories of the Guangdong opera hold that the Red Junk Companies were organized into the Hung Fa Wui Goon (Red Flower Union) in the 1730s by northern opera and Siu Lam (Shaolin) practitioner Cheung Ng, known by the nickname Tan Sao Ng (Dispersing Arm Ng). It thus far remains uncertain how the wing chun kuen art was transmitted to or was developed aboard the Red Junks. By the mid 1800s, however, it rested with several members of the company, including Wong Wah-Bo, Leung Yee-Tai, Painted Face Kam, and Go Lo Chung.

More information on the Red Junk performers can be found in the records of the Pan Nam Weng Chun system. These records reportedly come from the ancestral tablet of the Lok family, two of whom were said to have learned wing chun kuen from Painted Face Kam.

This account held in part that during the mid-19th century Yip Man-Sun (the Ching general of Guangdong and Guangxi provinces) was sent to smash the anti-Ching rebellions of Lee Man-Mao and Chan Hoi. In so doing, General Yip destroyed the opera theaters and outlawed the performances. This effectively ended their revolutionary movement until the 1860s when Sun Wah and Kwong Din-Hing, along with performers Wong Wah-Bo, Leung Yee-Tai, Painted Face Kam, and others formed the Baat Hop Wui Goon (Eight-Harmony Union) and re-opened the opera.

黃
華
寶

Wong Wah-Bo

Wong Wah-Bo was said to have been a native of Gulao village in Guangdong province's Heshan County. Strong and powerful, Wong played the roles of Mo Sang (Wu Sheng, the male martial lead) in the opera. These characters, such as the mischievous Monkey King, required a very high level of martial arts skill and knowledge of numerous and dynamic boxing and weapons sets. Wong was reportedly renowned for his performance of General Kwan and for his skill with the six-and-a-half-point pole. Wong is often implied to have been the *dai sihing* (senior-most classmate) of the Red Junk performers and is sometimes said to have helped with their instruction. By the mid-1870s, Wong had retired from the opera to Foshan. There he taught the Imperial constable, Fok Bo-Chuen, and fellow Gulao native, Leung Jan, who ran the Kuaizi (Chopstick) Street pharmacy.

大花面錦

Painted Face Kam

Dai Fa Min Kam (Painted Face Kam) is also sometimes referred to as San Kam (New Kam), and Yik Kam in different branches. He was said to have been quick and agile. Kam's nickname came from his Opera role of the Dai Fa Min (Painted Face), which required highly exaggerated make-up. As the Dai Fa Min, Kam's roles ranged from martial, to the comedic Chao (Chou, a clown-like role) to the antagonistic Ching (Jing). Kam was said to have begun teaching at roughly the same time as Wong Wah-Bo. His students included Fok Bo-Chuen in Foshan and Fung Siu-Ching, who worked as a military marshal in the nearby city of Guangzhou.

Leung Yee-Tai and Tall Chung

Leung Yee-Tai assisted Wong Wah-Bo in the teaching of Dr. Leung Jan, who went on to become the famed subject of novels and later, movies. Go Lo Chung (Tall Chung), on the other hand, taught his son-in-law, Siu Li-Chung.

Yuen Kay-San

Yuen Kay-San Jongsi, founder of the system. Foshan, mid 1900s.

Yuen Kay-San, also named Gwok-Wu, was born in 1889 in Foshan. Being the fifth son of his family, he was commonly called Yuen Lo Jia (Yuen the Fifth).

At a very young age, Yuen Kay-San and his elder brother Yuen Chai-Wan demonstrated great interest in and aptitude for the martial arts. Their father, Yuen Chong-Ming, was a wealthy merchant who owned a fireworks store on Zhenbei road.

阮奇山

Wing chun kuen masters at the time commanded a very high price for their instruction. Wanting to encourage his sons, Yuen Chong-Ming spent a small fortune to engage the renowned Fok Bo-Chuen in order to teach them the skills of wing chun kuen.

Studies Under Fok Bo-Chuen

Fok Bo-Chuen, sometimes rendered as Kwok Bo-Chuen, learned his wing chun kuen from Wong Wah-Bo and Painted Face Kam in the city of Foshan. There he served as a ngao moon bo tao (Imperial constable) during the end of the Ching dynasty.

霍保全

Renowned for his remarkable depth of martial knowledge and wing chun kuen skill, in some accounts, Fok was also said to have been particularly skilled in the use of the double knives.

Yuen Kay-San studied under Fok Bo-Chuen intensely for many years. Eventually, through hard work and determination, he learned all Fok Bo-Chuen had to teach (including the fist forms, the dummy sets, the pole, the knives, and the darts). Yuen Kay-San also succeeded in developing the devastating power of the iron sand palm.

Although he had developed a phenomenal foundation under the guidance of Fok Bo-Chuen, Yuen was still eager for more knowledge. This quest eventually led him to Fung Siu-Ching.

Studies Under Fung Siu-Ching

馮
少
青

Fung Siu-Ching was a native of Shunde, Guangdong who learned from Painted Face Kam in the city of Guangzhou, where he later worked as an Imperial marshal. He was also said to have served as a guard for the Sichuan Governor during the final years of the Ching dynasty.

An alternate account suggested that Fung Siu-Ching originally came from a province to the north and learned wing chun kuen from Ah Kam in Zhaoqing before moving northwest to work in Sichuan.

According to the verbal accounts of the Siu Lam weng chun style (which descends from Fung Siu-Ching's early teachings), Fung worked as a tailor's apprentice in Foshan as a youth. One day, opera performer San Kam came to the shop where Fung worked, seeking to commission new costumes. Fung Siu-Ching, a foul tempered youth, started a confrontation with the seemingly harmless opera performer. It took only three tumbles into the dirt for the youth to learn his lesson. Seeing Kam's skill, Fung Siu-Ching desperately wanted to become his disciple. Following a probationary period that required Fung, in part, to apply Kam's "Painted Face" make-up prior to each performance, the opera member finally accepted the dedicated youth as his student.

In his early years, Fung Siu-Ching taught the Siu Lam Weng Chun style to his son, Fung Ting, and to disciples Dong Suen, the Lo brothers, Dong Jik, and others. His students were said to have spread the style in Guangdong (where many protected local villages from bandits and gained the nickname "Kings of the Long Poles") and into Southeast Asian nations such as Thailand, Malaysia, and Singapore.

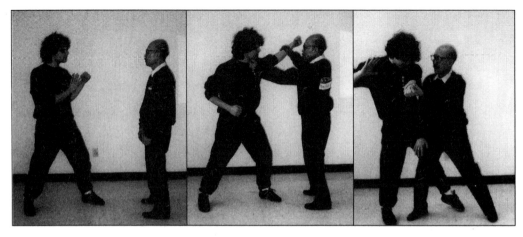

Antony Casella faces Ngo Lui-Kay sifu. When Antony shoots forward and strikes, Ngo sifu counters with a punch before sealing Antony's center and striking with a closing shoulder technique and punch to the groin.

There are a few differing tales that relate how Yuen Kay-San gained introduction to Fung Siu-Ching. One recounts that Yuen Chong-Ming, thinking his son needed more knowledge, arranged the meeting. Another relates that Yuen Kay-San met Fung Siu-Ching while paying a courtesy call to a relative who had once been governor of Sichuan province (to whom Fung had served as a guard). A third variation maintains that Fok Bo-Chuen directed Yuen Kay-San to his classmate, Fung Siu-Ching, when Fok realized he had nothing else to teach the young man. A final version states that Yuen Kay-San, Ma Jung-Yiu, and others invited Fung to Foshan to teach them after having heard of his great reputation.

When Yuen Kay-San approached Fung Siu-Ching for lessons, Fung was approximately 70 years of age, and was about to retire. Initially, Fung felt that the youth already had a strong foundation and told Yuen that there was little he could do to improve it. Yuen Kay-San was not so easily put off, however, and asked to touch hands with the old marshal. Whether due to the advantages of youth or the veteran guile of Fung, at first Yuen appeared to gain the upper-hand. Fung gave ground until his back was pressed up against a wall. Although seemingly without options, Fung startled the youth by quickly applying an explosive shoulder strike that sent Yuen tumbling. Realizing there was something to be added to Yuen Kay-San's training, Fung Siu-Ching agreed to move into the Yuen family estate and teach him martial arts.

Studying alongside Yuen Kay-San at the time were his elder brother Yuen Chai-Wan, Ma Jung-Yiu (pharmacist son of Ma Bok-Leung), Jiu Gan-Heung (son of the owner of Go Sing Hall), Lo Hao-Po (of the Ying Joi Restaurant), Lee Gwang-Po (of Nanhai), Au Si (of the Kuaizi Street butcher shop), and Leung Yan (of Huahong road).

Already accomplished in the wing chun kuen of Fok Bo-Chuen, Yuen Kay-San's education under Fung Siu-Ching consisted of advanced application and close-body fighting (including seizing and holding, counter seizing and holding, finger breaking, etc.). Yuen was also said to have honed his dummy, pole, and flying dart techniques under Fung's guidance.

Fung Siu-Ching's skill was widely regarded throughout the wing chun kuen family, even in other branches. In the article My Father—Yip Man, Yip Chun named Fung Siu-Ching alongside Wong Fei-Hung (of Hung family boxing), Cheung Hung-Sing (of Choy Lee Fut boxing), and Leung Jan as one of the famous masters of southern boxing from Foshan. Fung was especially praised for his skill with the six-and-a-half-point pole. Yip Ching, in his video on the wing chun kuen pole, recounted a story about Fung Siu-Ching exchanging pole techniques with Dr. Leung Jan at a local smokehouse. Moy Yat, in the essay Ving Tsun Six-and-a-Half-Point Pole further wrote that he once asked his teacher, Yip Man about the quality of pole techniques in Foshan. While Yip could not say for certain who possessed the highest skill, he did remark that Fung Siu-Ching had the strongest fingers he had ever seen.

Fung Siu-Ching lived, taught, and was cared for at the Yuen family estate until he passed away at the age of 73. Yuen Kay-San and his classmates officiated at the old marshal's funeral. Following their training with Fung Siu-Ching, the Yuen brothers took different paths. In 1936, Yuen Chai-Wan (who was also known as Dao Pei Chai or Pock Skin Chai), moved to Vietnam. In some accounts this was following a duel where he killed his opponent and needed to leave Foshan. In Vietnam Yuen Chai-Wan (pronounced locally as Nguyen Te-Cong) taught wing chun kuen (Vinh Xuan) at the Nanhai and Shunde Expatriates Association before later moving south where he passed away in 1960.

Yuen Kay-San stayed in Foshan and worked on developing his wing chun kuen. Throughout his lessons, Yuen had always taken copious notes. He spent time analyzing the scientific principles of wing chun kuen and became one of the first to document its formal concepts. Linking together and refining all the knowledge he had acquired, Yuen developed a complete understanding of wing chun kuen and went on to found remarkable methods and principles encompassing its forms and functions.

Yuen Kay-San did not boast of his skills nor seek out confrontation. Instead, he used his abilities only to defend himself, his property, and for practice. Although he did everything possible to avoid it, from time to time circumstances arose which forced Yuen into combat. Many of these matches became the subjects of articles written by local journalists such as Au Soi-Jee, the famed author of *Mr. Jan of Foshan*.

Georgia Dow launches a surprise attack at Ngo sifu, who responds with a grasping arm and hanging punch while hooking her leg with his own. Georgia tries to retreat and create enough space for a counter but Ngo sifo chases her step with another grasping arm hanging punch, using an angle horse to attack her leg.

Taming the Mantis

Yiu Lok-Gong of tong long kuen (mantis boxing) was sent to Foshan from Shanghai by his famous teacher in order to organize the town's Martial Arts Association. The mantis boxer was famed for his leg techniques and was said to be able to send a large rice bag flying across the room with a single kick. Upon his arrival, regional pride caused tempers to flare and challenges to be made. Eventually, a fight was arranged between Yiu Lok-Gong and a wing chun boxer.

On the day of the fight, Yuen Kay-San came to observe and sat near-by, slippers dangling from his feet. When the time came, however, Yiu's opponent was nowhere to be found. Yiu had heard that Yuen was a wing chun kuen practitioner of considerable skill and turned to him as a suitable replacement. Yuen was not interested in such contests, and refused the mantis boxer. Yiu would not take no for an answer, however, and eventually launched an attack at Yuen anyway. Yuen leapt to his feet, without time to even properly place his slippers, and quickly dissolved the attack. Yiu retreated slightly and tried to follow up the attack, but Yuen chased his steps, sticking to his arms and jamming his famous legs. Without having to resort to his more deadly skills, Yuen pressed the mantis practitioner until he ran out of room, his back against a barred door. No longer able to retreat, and under Yuen's complete control, Yiu was forced to submit. Yiu was impressed by both Yuen Kay-San's skills and his mercy in not harming him, and considered adding wing chun kuen's hand techniques to his own system.

There are several different accounts of this famed confrontation. One version, in which Yiu Lok-Gong ambushed Yuen Kay-San while Yuen was lying on a bed in a smokehouse, was published in a pulp novel in the 1960s.

A Pickpocket at the Train Station

Yuen Kay-San was at the train station one day when he saw a pickpocket relieve a man of his purse. Yuen hurried over to the man, told him what had happened, and pointed out the robber. The pickpocket, incensed over being exposed, ran toward Yuen Kay-San to attack. Yuen Kay-San, sensing the strike towards his flank, launched a quick but powerful side butting palm to intercept and counter the blow. The robber collapsed to the ground instantly and was left drooling all over himself, knocked senseless by the single strike.

Pole Fighting

Yuen Kay-San was also famed for his duels with the long pole. In his 1920s book, *Six-and-a-Half-Point Pole*, Au Soi-Jee named Yuen Kay-San, alongside such famed ancestors as Wong Wah-Bo, as a major contributor to the wing chun kuen pole techniques. The book also related the story of Yuen defeating Wong Faat-Leung in a test of pole skill.

Another story tells of a warrior monk from Jiangxi province who came to Foshan to compare pole techniques with Yuen Kay-San. Yuen refused many times but the monk was relentless and eventually Yuen agreed. These types of altercations could often result in critical injury or even death, so wavers were drafted and the fight was set to take place at the Foshan "Palace of Ten Thousand Years Longevity." During the course of the fight Yuen succeeded in knocking the monk's pole away, leaving him defenseless. With the monk's life hanging in the balance, Yuen declared the fight over, proving again not only his skill but also his morality.

In one exciting telling of this story, the encounter was fought with poles of solid iron.

Leading the Quiet Life

Although he occasionally worked as a lawyer for the government of Foshan, Yuen Kay-San did little else with his time but practice wing chun kuen.

Many of the wing chun kuen practitioners of the time were the sons of wealthy merchants and traveled in similar circles. Although from different branches, Yuen Kay-San would often spend his time discussing wing chun kuen with them at the local tea and smokehouses. Among his close friends were Ng Jung-So, Cheung Bo, and his neighbor, Yip Man. Others, outside wing chun kuen, included Hung family boxing practitioner, Leung Yum-Tong, as well as Dr. Lee Gwong-Hoi.

Aside from this, Yuen Kay-San was a deeply private man and tried as much as possible to keep his knowledge of wing chun kuen to himself. He did not open a school, engage in public displays, and did not even reveal his background to acquaintances.

Because of his private nature, over the generations many conflicting accounts have arisen about Yuen Kay-San. Knowing of his reputation, but not his history, many of the early pulp novel writers and others have attempted to link him to the better-known branches of wing chun kuen. Stories were passed along casting him as a student of Leung Jan, Chan Wah-Shun, and/or Ng Jung-So, and contained numerous other inaccuracies. Some of the authors later attempted to set the record straight, such as Au Soi-Jee who wrote *The Biography of Yuen Kay-San*. However, Yuen Kay-San so deeply disliked publicity that he requested the book not be published. Thus, although Yuen Jo-Tong and others have done much in recent times to clarify his background, to this day many tales still confuse the history of Yuen Kay-San.

Cheung Bo

張
保

One of Yuen Kay-San's close friends, Cheung Bo, worked as a chef at Tien Hoi, a local restaurant off Kuaizi Street. Cheung was a large and powerful man who taught wing chun kuen to a small group of fellow staff members at night when the establishment was closed.

Although his exact lineage remains uncertain, Cheung Bo was said to have learned his wing chun kuen from Nationalist army doctor Wai Yuk-Sang, who was rumored to have studied under Fung Siu-Ching's pupil Au Si. Due to similarities in content and organization, it has also been suggested that an ancestral connection may exist with the san sao system passed down in Gulao village by the famed Dr. Leung Jan.

Cheung Bo was renowned for his fighting skills, which he reportedly used to keep even the raucous young martial artists who frequented the restaurant in line. One of his students at the time was a young boy named Sum Nung.

Sum Nung

 Although born in Peru in 1926, Sum Nung was brought to Foshan, China as an infant by relatives so that the family name would continue in its land of origin. When the Japanese invaded, however, Sum's family lost contact with their relatives in Peru and over night went from a life of prosperity to one of poverty. Determined to help support his family, Sum took a job at Tien Hoi restaurant.

Sum Nung was often forced to defend himself against local bullies which eventually led him to seek wing chun kuen instruction from fellow staff member, Cheung Bo. The chef, seeing a great deal of determination in the child, agreed to take him as a student. Although the style was simple, it built in him a very solid foundation.

Sum Nung, grandmaster of
Yuen Kay-San Wing Chun Kuen. Guangzhou, late '60s.

Early Encounters
Cheung Bo encouraged Sum Nung to test his skills and learn from his experience. One day, Sum Nung was accosted by a man armed with double watermelon choppers. While Cheung stood relaxed against a wall a short distance away, Sum was forced to defend himself empty handed. As the deadly blades whipped by, the youngster tried to protect himself as much as he could but received several nasty cuts along his arms. Luckily, he managed to find an opening and countered with lightning speed. Sum's skillful response sent the man's knives tumbling through the air, forcing the gathered onlookers to scatter for cover.

The Skills of Yuen Kay-San
Yuen Kay-San would often drop by Tien Hoi to visit his friend Cheung Bo and take tea. After dining at the restaurant, he would sometimes remain behind and watch the staff practice their wing chun kuen. While observing, he would stay quiet, never commenting nor criticizing. Over time, however, he grew to admire the dedication of Sum Nung and eventually asked Cheung if he could take over the youth's instruction. Cheung, respecting the tremendous quality of Yuen Kay-San's wing chun kuen, and knowing that he had already taught the youth all he could, happily agreed and soon introduced Sum Nung to Yuen Kay-San.

Sum Nung was hesitant at first. He had been learning from Cheung Bo for a few years and saw Yuen Kay-San, older and quite slender, as a stark contrast to his young and powerful teacher. This feeling led him to question Yuen's skills. Yuen, seeing in Sum Nung a great desire and potential, was willing to indulge the youth. Promising that the youth could use all that he knew, and vowing only to defend in return, Yuen Kay-San invited Sum Nung to touch hands with him.

Sum Nung, his curiosity piqued, took up Yuen's challenge. Sum attacked with all his youthful vigor and the full range of his skills, but each time Yuen Kay-San calmly intercepted his techniques and after only one or two movements left Sum unable to continue. Realizing that Yuen's skills were of the highest level, Sum quickly became his student.

In one dramatic account of this story, Yuen Kay-San reportedly placed eggs in all of his pockets and told Sum Nung that if he could so much as crack a single one, he would admit defeat and be on his way. Needless to say, following the encounter, Sum Nung was amazed to see the old man pull every single egg from his pockets, each completely intact.

Sum Nung's Training
Over the years, Yuen Kay-San and Sum Nung spent much time together, constantly practicing wing chun kuen. From Yuen, Sum Nung learned the hand forms, the wooden dummy, the pole, the double knives, and worked at developing his sticking hands and fighting skills.

When Yuen Kay-San was unavailable, Sum Nung would drill with Wong Jing. Wong had previously learned wing chun kuen from a student of Dr. Leung Jan's named Lai Yeung-Yin, but also spent some time following Yuen Kay-San. When not practicing, Sum would sit beside Yuen Kay-San while Yuen discussed wing chun kuen's concepts. Under Yuen's guidance, Sum continued to refine and polish his wing chun kuen, developing an intelligent and practical style as simple and efficient as it was well rounded and effective.

A Match with Dai Lik Yiu Choi
Sometimes, Yuen Kay-San would take Sum Nung for friendly tests of skill. On one such occasion, Yuen arranged for Sum to have a match with a friend known as Dai Lik Yiu Choi (Big and Powerful Yiu Choi). When the match began, Sum quickly gained the advantage and knocked Yiu to the floor. When Sum reached out his hand to help Yiu Choi up, however, Yiu took the opportunity to strike Sum Nung. Yiu Choi then declared the match a draw.

Another version of this story holds that the match took place late at night near a very large, hot soup pot. During the course of the contest, Sum Nung tossed Yiu Choi near the pot. Sum Nung stopped his technique to prevent Yiu Choi from being injured and Yiu Choi took the chance to counter.

Wai Yuk-Sang's Test
Alongside his wing chun kuen training, Sum Nung also studied Chinese medicine from Dr. Wai Yuk-Sang. When Dr. Wai heard that Sum had been learning from Yuen Kay-San, he became curious. Wanting to see what the young man had accomplished, the doctor asked to touch hands with him. Sum was in a quandary. On the one hand, he had the reputation of Yuen Kay-San to consider, while on the other, he had to make sure he didn't jeopardize his medical training. Instinct settled the issue when Dr. Wai attacked and Sum automatically detained the arm and lightly touched his medicine teacher on the cheek. Suitably impressed, Wai Yuk-Sang urged Sum Nung to study hard and thoroughly master the skills of Yuen's wing chun kuen.

Guangdong
Foshan & Surroundings

Qingyuan

Guangzhou

Zhaoqing Foshan

Shunde

Heshan Shenzhen

Hong Kong

Macau

South China Sea

Moving to Guangzhou
By the mid-1940s, Sum Nung had gained a great reputation for his wing chun kuen fighting skills in Foshan. Among his acquaintances were several of Yuen Kay-San's friends, such as Leung Yum-Tong and Yip Man, as well as Yip's early students like Gwok Fu and Lun Gai, who would drop by Tien Hoi restaurant on occasion.

Over the years, Sum Nung's attention came to be completely consumed by wing chun kuen and medicine. By the late 1940s, when it began to effect his work, his employer let him go.

At just over 20 years of age, Sum Nung decided to move to the nearby provincial capitol of Guangzhou to pursue his medical career. In the early days, he supported himself by teaching wing chun kuen and providing medical services to members of the Iron Workers Union, Restaurant Workers Union, Five Metals Union, and other guilds. Among his earliest students was his uncle, Sum Jee (sometimes referred to as Sum Hei). Sum Jee was a famed local Hung ga kuen practitioner. When he met up with his young nephew, however, he was amazed by the skills of wing chun kuen and soon began studying the art.

Although Sum Nung, like Yuen Kay-San, did not boast of his abilities nor seek out confrontation, he did on occasion have friendly tests of skill with practitioners of other martial arts. Although he seldom spoke of the encounters out of respect for his opponents' reputations, it is said that in them he never met with failure and his reputation in Guangzhou grew steadily.

Over the years, Sum Nung visited Yuen Kay-San as much as possible. During Sum Nung's absence Yuen continued his relationships with other wing chun kuen practitioners. One of his closest friends remained Yip Man, especially after the Yip family estate was damaged by fire during the Japanese occupation and the Yuen family helped fight the blaze and provide shelter thereafter. Their friendship continued until Yip moved to Hong Kong in late 1949, just prior to the rise of Communist China.

Sum Nung's Promise
Following the formation of the People's Republic of China, Yuen Kay-San's health began to deteriorate. During one of his visits to Foshan, Yuen told Sum Nung that he was afraid that when he died, his name and his contributions to wing chun kuen would be forgotten. Sum Nung promised his teacher that this would not come to pass.

When Yuen Kay-San passed away from illness in November 1956, in keeping with his promise, Sum Nung named his art Yuen Kay-San wing chun kuen in honor and memory of his teacher.

Life in Guangzhou
When Sum Nung returned to Guangzhou he began working in a local clinic. He continued to teach Yuen Kay-San wing chun kuen, but due to the politics that followed the Communist rise to power and the subsequent Cultural Revolution, he did so privately, not wanting to attract too much attention.

A Knife and a Kick

During the Cultural Revolution Sum Nung was attacked one day by a knife-wielding assailant. Sum managed to deflect most of the attack with a half-dispersing-half-wing technique, but the blade was sufficiently long to nonetheless stab slightly into his chest. Knowing that hesitation could prove fatal, Sum quickly yanked his assailant to the side and simultaneously struck out with a heart piercing kick to the man's waist. The attacker limped away, badly injured from the devastating strike.

Rene Ritchie thrusts quickly at Ngo sifu. Intercepting with a half-dispersing-half-wing technique, Ngo sifu pulls his opponent into a powerful heart-piercing kick.

Iron Arms

Sum Nung is sometimes referred to by the nickname Tiet Bei (Iron Arms) due to the explosive short power he can generate from his forearms with techniques such as the barring arm and center cleaving arm. One encounter that helped fuel the nickname also occurred during the Cultural Revolution. In those days, Communist China did not support the traditional martial arts and many practitioners were harassed, persecuted, and sometimes even killed. It was under these conditions that grandmaster Sum Nung was reportedly set upon one day by several members of the Red Guard. In the course of defending himself, Sum Nung broke the arm of one of his attackers with a penetrating barring arm technique and managed to emerge unscathed.

The Wrestler's Challenge

Sum Nung was introduced by Wong Jing to a national sut gao (shuai jiao, wrestling) champion who was curious as to the effectiveness of wing chun kuen. The wrestler believed that he could withstand one or two strikes and then take the fight to the ground where he would surely dominate. Sum Nung invited him to give it a try and they met one day behind closed doors in a small hall lined with benches against the walls. Following the principles of wing chun kuen, Sum remained neutral in his ready posture and waited for the wrestler to act. When the wrestler shot in, Sum joined with his bridges, uprooted the wrestler, and sent him tumbling into the nearby benches. This occurred a few more times until the wrestler, suitably impressed with the skills of wing chun kuen, expressed the desire to become a student. It was his hope to use wing chun kuen to bridge the gap between his wrestling and long range martial arts.

Grandmaster Sum Nung stands with some of his students. From left:
Ngo Liu-Kay, Sum Nung, Leung Da-Chiu, Dong Chuen-Kam. (Guangzhou, late 1960s.)

Expanding the Art

Over the years, teaching only those whom he felt were upright and trustworthy, grandmaster Sum Nung went on to train many outstanding students. In addition to Sum Jee, Sum Nung's students from the late 1940s to early 1960s included former dragon shape boxer Lao Lo-Wai, as well as Kwok Jin-Fun, Pan Chao, and Leung King-Chiu (know as Dai Chiu, who moved to Hong Kong around 1970 and later to the United States).

From the mid-1960s, his students included Ngo Lui-Kay (who relocated to Canada in 1982), Fu family internal stylist Kwok Wan-Ping (who established the Guangzhou Wing Chun and Tai Gik (taiji) School in Hong Kong in the late 1960s), and Lee Chi-Yiu (who moved to Hong Kong in the early 1970s). Around 1980, Sum Nung also taught performer Tam Heung-Ming, known by the opera name Siu Siu Gai.

Other students of Sum Nung such as Dr. Wong Tiet-Wai (Teddy Wong, who moved to New York in the early 1970s) and Tom Wong (who relocated to Los Angeles) helped introduce the style to the United States. Also in the Los Angeles area, Chu Sau-Lei (Robert Chu), student of Kwan Jong-Yuen, preserves a lineage descending from Kwok Jin-Fen and Pan Chao, through Chan Mei-Shun and Wong Fen.

Several of Kwok Wan-Ping's early students also brought the art to North America, including Dr. Tse Chung-Fai in British Columbia, Chow Gwok-Tai in Ontario, and Lee Chung-Ming in Virginia. Lo Kuen-Hung (Henry Lo), who learned the art from Lee Chi-Yiu, also helped establish it in Ontario.

Kwok Wan-Ping sifu moved to Hong Kong in the late 1960s and established the Guangzhou Wing Chun and Taiji Institute.

In Australia, students of Sum Nung such as Cheng Hung-Chuen (Oliver Cheng), have helped spread the art in the southern hemisphere.

Sum Nung has also endeavored to help keep wing chun kuen "in the family," sharing his insights with Yuen Kay-San's grandson, Jo-Tong. In keeping with a pledge he made his first teacher, Sum Nung has also taught Cheung Bo's son, Ah Chut. In addition, Sum Nung is passing along the art to his own children.

Sum Nung's Legacy

Grandmaster Sum Nung has continued to develop and refine his art over the decades, concentrating on practical application. This has led to his system being recognized as one of the most effective in China.

Today, due to the hard work and determination of grandmaster Sum Nung and of his students and descendants, the art of Yuen Kay-San continues to move forward and establish itself internationally.

Lee Chi-Tiu sifu, shown here demonstrating the cultivating arm hanging punch, followed to Hong Kong in the early 1970s.

Grandmaster Sum Nung, students, family, and friends pose on the occasion of his 48th birthday. Sum Nung (center) is flanked to the left by Dong Chuen-Kam, and to the right by Ngo Lui-Kay, among others.

Ngo Lui-Kay and classmate Tam Heung-Ming (better known as opera performer Siu Siu Gai) take in the sites during Tam's visit to Canada in the early 1980s.

PART TWO

基本點

Fundamentals

CHAPTER 3

Concepts of Wing Chun Kuen

Jn modern martial art terms the name wing chun kuen means that the practitioner must actively work towards the continual rebirth of the system's fighting skills. This shows that the art is alive, vibrant, always growing—not stiff, mechanical, or dead. Thus it is the job of every practitioner to make the seeds of wing chun kuen burst forth in application. These seeds are the *yiu dim* (important points) or concepts.

Wing chun kuen is not a technical style, it is a conceptual system. More than a set combination of poetic movements it is an ingenious index and guide to the core principles of southern Chinese martial arts. The ideas are what are important since from them come the many individual applications and implications. Rather than forcing practitioners to spend vast amounts of time repeating large numbers of fixed patterns it allows them to economically practice a few root points that can be applied in almost limitless ways. This maximizes training time and means that the art is not bound to material but can develop and grow as far as the practitioner's intelligence and devotion allows.

The Meridian Line

The *jee ng sien* (meridian line) is behind many of the major principles of wing chun kuen. Like most Chinese martial art concepts it is deep in meaning and can be viewed in several different ways. First, it defines the line that vertically bisects the practitioner's body from the crown-point, through the eyes, chest, and dan tian, all the way down to the central point between the feet. Second, it indicates the same line through an opponent's body. Third, it encompasses the most direct root between the practitioner's center and that of the opponent. In wing chun kuen a practitioner gains the advantage by aligning his or her structure on the meridian, striking the opponent's center, and dominating the line between the two.

Rene approaches Georgia and she immediately raises her arms. As Rene begins a swing, Georgia strikes down the meridian line. Due to the direct route of her attack, she arrives first. Interrupting his assault, Georgia maintains dominance of the mutual line and quickly follows up.

With the structure aligned on the central meridian, the wing chun kuen practitioner ensures that as much of his or her ground-derived power and body mass as possible goes directly into the opponent. Positions can also be maintained and movements executed with a minimum of muscular tension, allowing for the relaxation that leads to greater acceleration. At the same time the initial alignment is already in place for dispersing, controlling, and otherwise dealing with an opponent's force. This minimizes the amount of movement necessary to deal with attacks, greatly improving reaction time.

Striking into an opponent's center makes disrupting their body structure easier. Thus, turning away from, wedging into, or otherwise dissolving the force of an attack requires much more effort on an opponent's part. Furthermore, many of an opponent's more vulnerable areas are located on the meridian line. Attacking these can lead to a faster and more economical end to an altercation.

By effectively dominating the meridian line between oneself and one's opponent it ensures the practitioner of quick and direct attacks while at the same time forcing opponents to travel around them, reducing the integrity of their own techniques. In addition, like an open fan, the practitioner has placed himself at the center of a circle and can fully engage all limbs immediately without significant body displacement. Meanwhile, the opponent must travel the outside of the circle and when flanked can not make use of most of their tools without first re-positioning, thus further slowing response time.

The 12 Methods

The *sup yee faat* (12 methods) are the basis of wing chun kuen. They are at the same time the simplest and yet the most profound of Yuen Kay-San's written principles. Rich in meaning, the 12 methods provide a gateway to deeper understanding of the style. Following are brief explanations of each of the 12 methods.

1. *Dap* (to join two bridges). The first method deals with the establishment of contact with the opponent. Without contact, there cannot be any transmission of power, defensively or offensively. Thus, joining is almost always the first method used in any application of wing chun kuen.

2. *Jeet* (to intercept, to cut-off). It is said in wing chun kuen that the opponent should only be able to make one or two movements before they are left unable to continue. This method deals with the nullification of an opponent's current techniques, the cutting off of future techniques (combination or linked attacks) before they can begin, and the shutting down of an opponent's offense entirely.

3. *Chum* (to sink down). Gravity pulls us toward the earth. Recognizing this, wing chun kuen uses gravity to its advantage, sinking down for stability, to disperse force, destroy an opponent's structure, and to generate power.

4. *Biu* (to dart, to thrust). Wing chun kuen motions are not tense, inflexible, or plodding in application. When in motion, the arms fly like darts into the opponent, relaxed, fast, accurate, and with precisely focused power.

Rene remains relaxed and centered while Georgia is poised to attack. Georgia launches a thrusting punch and Rene intercepts with a dispersing arm thrusting punch. Georgia raises her leg in an attempt to follow up. Feeling the motion, Rene changes to a grasping arm. Just as Georgia is about to kick, Rene pulls her off balance, leaving her open and cutting off any further offence on her part.

5. *Chi* (to stick, to adhere). In close proximity the hand can be quicker than the eye, feeling movement before it is seen. Once the bridges are joined, wing chun kuen sticks to the opponent, using the connection to gather information and enhance reaction time. Like glutinous rice, however, wing chun kuen sticks only when the force is right.

6. *Mo* (to touch, to feel). An opponent does not stay still. When in contact wing chun kuen continuously feels for the center to maintain optimal positioning. With feeling guiding the way, power can be used precisely and economically.

7. *Tong* (to press). Sometimes linear force is too easily understood by an opponent to be effective. Thus, wing chun kuen pushes with a cascading force, like an iron on clothing. It moves power from upward down, side to side, or in other directions to uproot and displace an opponent.

8. *Dong* (to swing). Change is at the heart of wing chun kuen. If an opponent resists moving to the right, change and move him or her left. If he or she resists a pull, apply a push. In essence, an opponent's own reactions are used against him or her.

9. *Tun* (to swallow, to take possession). Rather than resisting an opponent or fighting force with force, wing chun kuen swallows power. This subtle method of diffusion denies an opponent the sensory perception that an oppositional defense might and can lead them into a disadvantageous position.

10. *Chit* (to slice). For an opponent to be effectively dealt with his or her structure must be disrupted on initial contact. Thus, wing chun kuen cuts into an opponent like a knife carving meat. This immediate uprooting and destabilization makes it difficult for an opponent to take the offense and gives the practitioner an opportunity to quickly follow up.

11. *Tao* (to steal, to pilfer). When an opportunity presents itself, it is taken. During movement, an opponent can carelessly or unavoidably create openings in his or her defense and expose vulnerable targets. Unprotected areas are exploited and unguarded doors are entered like a thief in the night.

12. *Lao* (to leak). Similar to stealing, leaking deals more with a situation in which contact already exists. As an opponent moves, the wing chun boxer follows along, feels for the opening, and then runs in like water leaking through a hole in the roof.

Some combine *tao* and *lao* into one method and add an additional composite method—*kao saat* (detain and kill).

Tactical Advice

Tactical advice is passed down in the Yuen Kay-San system through sets of four character rhyming couplets such as the *yiu ku* (important rhymed formulae) and the similar *faat mun* (methodologies).

要訣 The wing chun kuen formulae relate that as force comes, it should be received and kept. It is never resisted or knocked away but accepted and adhered to. As force goes, it is accompanied and added to. When a loss of contact occurs, or the body is crossed, a practitioner is advised to charge straight down the meridian line.

If the root is stable, the fight will be stable. When turning, the body and hands act together. When an opponent moves, he or she will have already lost his or her center of balance and can be disrupted more easily. When faced with overly active opponents, the wing chun kuen practitioner remains calm and centered, physically and mentally. Energy is conserved while an opponent is left to tire on his or her own until such time as engagement is necessary.

Wing chun kuen does not prepare or plan ahead of time and stubbornly enact these plans regardless of circumstance. It attacks according to current conditions and is alive and ever changing. Every offense is a defense and each defense is an offense. When changes are done skillfully, a practitioner can achieve twice the results with only half the effort.

The eyes are directed where the intention and mind are directed and the gaze is attentive. When reacting to peripheral motion, if something is encountered it should be received and kept. If nothing is encountered, the motion may have been a deception and the practitioner should cleave the center to intercept any true attacks.

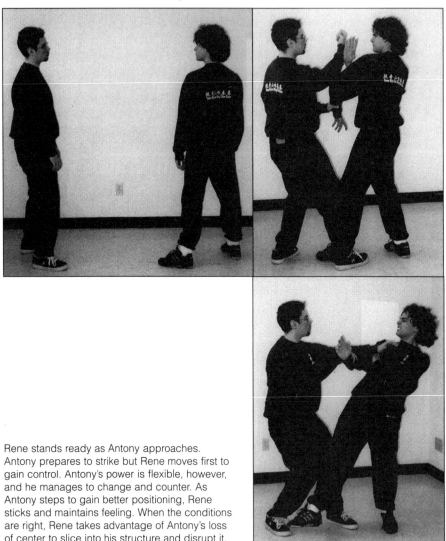

Rene stands ready as Antony approaches. Antony prepares to strike but Rene moves first to gain control. Antony's power is flexible, however, and he manages to change and counter. As Antony steps to gain better positioning, Rene sticks and maintains feeling. When the conditions are right, Rene takes advantage of Antony's loss of center to slice into his structure and disrupt it.

Wing chun boxers must learn to apply their power in the most advantageous way, moving with the wind rather then against it. Its power is soft, calm, and quiet. Practitioners must therefore have faith in themselves to use it. Soft is employed to overcome hard but both hard and soft are combined in use. Enemies are fought fiercely and attacks may be initiated in order to gain control. Once an initial attack is made, it is followed in succession until the target is no more.

Training Principles

 Sets of five character rhyming couplets pass along training principles in the Yuen Kay-San system. They include the *yiu jee* (important ideas) and the *ching yan* (introductions). These sets relate to working hard, being healthy, studying, being nimble, using the eyes, and being first.

When studying the martial arts, practitioners are encouraged to practice hard, learn to their utmost, and fully realize the principles involved.

To maintain health, one should eat well and moderate lust. Furthermore, it is said the heart should be quiet and *hei* (qi, breath/intrinsic energy) should be conserved. The mind must be clear and the body and arms should be properly aligned. Strength must be exacting in position, never overextended. It is aware, follows, and changes with feeling.

During training, the eyes should be angry and look straight forward. Changes should be explored through sticking with a partner. A teacher must correct these practices. When there is no teacher and no partner, a mirror and dummy should be used to aid in this pursuit and one must imagine an enemy is present.

Practitioners who are good can wait and see. Those who are not yet good must go test. It must be remembered that there is always someone better, so a practitioner cannot hold back. When an opportunity presents itself, it must be taken and followed up without pause. Action must be timely and decisive, because winning and losing can be decided right away.

In addition, practitioners are advised to follow the methods of the ancestors but to remember to adapt according to conditions. Lastly, it is said that if one works hard and trains hard, one is unlikely to meet with failure.

CHAPTER 4

Wing Chun Kuen Body Structure

Wing chun kuen *san ying* (body structure) strives to achieve several important goals. It works off simple, natural, geometric shapes that can be reflexively assumed and easily maintained, even during stressful situations like combat (where more complicated mechanics can break down). Utilizing the concepts of the meridian line, the body is positioned so that it closes off direct access, obstructing opponents before they begin (increasing the effort and time it takes to attack). This skeletal alignment also naturally disperses incoming force, reducing the need for muscle movement (making responses faster and less tiring). These enable the practitioner to work as little as possible while forcing the opponent to work as much as possible.

While each individual motion will have its own unique characteristics, there are several overall structural principles that can generally be applied to most movements. It should be remembered that positions are always relative and depend on the build of the individual involved.

The Lower Body

The lower body is often referred to as *ma*. Although frequently translated as "stance," *ma* is actually the word for "horse." This reveals a dynamic rather then static nature. In wing chun kuen the horse should actively clamp like flexible steel and move like the wheels of a cart. It is the connection between the ground (the source of power in Chinese martial arts) and the upper body. When standing it serves to root the practitioner to the ground. If an opponent pushes, he or she pushes the ground. If he or she pulls, he or she pulls the ground. When moving, the lower body functions like a spatula or a cow-pusher to disrupt, uproot, and send off an opponent.

1. Point the feet inward and grab with the toes. While standing, the feet are the ultimate connection between the body and the ground. The converging nature of the feet creates an internal rotation in the horse and aids in stability. The grabbing action of the toes helps with rooting.

The horse is like flexible steel

2. Lower the posture and clamp the knees. Lowering the posture aids stability and helps ensure a rooted horse. Clamping the knees involves rotating them inward and closing them to one-fist distance. This provides a solid, pyramid-like structure for training and can help in the channeling of power from the ground. The two work in concert, however, as the knees are brought close together not so much by horizontally pressing them in as by sinking the posture to adduct them.

3. Tuck the hips under and draw in the anus to join the upper and lower bodies together. This is important in order to create the connection between the ground and the torso and to project power through that connection. It also helps in promoting proper *hei* (qi) circulation and conservation by completing the microcosmic orbit.

The Upper Body

The upper body forms the link between the bridge arms and the horse. It should be sunken and relaxed. If it becomes tense, power will not be able to flow freely. When still the upper body is said to be like a standing crane. When in contact, the expansion and contraction of the torso (intercostals, chest, etc.) also works to generate and disperse certain forms of power.

1. Straighten the back. In general the back is kept vertical, leaning neither forward nor backward. This neutral posture is in keeping with wing chun kuen's concept of the center. In application, it works with the rest of the torso, expanding and contracting when expressing or receiving power.

2. Relax the chest and abdomen. The stomach and chest are not tensed but naturally relaxed and sunken. As wing chun kuen can boil down to a game of seconds and inches, the relaxed body can react more quickly and the sunken posture can provide a slight advantage in reach (keeping the body a little further back).

3. Straighten the head. Since the head can weigh a fair amount, having it droop forward or back can affect balance. With the head in line with the upper and lower body, uniformity of structure is maintained allowing for proper alignment when standing and moving.

The upper body is like a standing crane

The Bridge Arms

橋
手

Kiu sao (bridge arms), sometimes shortened to simply kiu (bridges) or *sao* (hands or arms), are so named in Southern Chinese martial arts because they are the most common tools used to make contact with an opponent. Thus, the arms form the bridge between the practitioner and their target. Like the torso, the bridges are relaxed and adaptable (moving, it is sometimes said, like swimming dragons.)

The arms are like swimming dragons

1. Hang the shoulders. The shoulders should remain relaxed. Tense shoulders will stop the transfer of power from the ground and cause the body to rely on localized arm power alone.

2. Close the elbows. Wing chun kuen does not flare the elbows but keeps them closed toward the meridian line. This means that in most situations, the elbows are kept down andclose to the body. The exact placement will vary depending on the situation. Keeping the elbow joint pointing down ensures a straight punch that is more difficult for an oppnent to turn with or deflect from the outside, or to jam or lock. Keeping the elbows in minimizes exposed areas, reducing the opponent's chance of stealing a strike. Furthermore, a flared elbow requires local arm muscle to maintain its structure. Closed elbows, on the other hand, put the entire body mass directly behind the punch. This allows the arm to remain relaxed and yet move with even greater power.

2. Extend the elbows. When the bridges go out the elbows are not restrained against the torso but move to a position roughly one-fist distance in front of the body. This is done both to increase the structural integrity of the arms and to prevent an opponent from using the bridges to lever the body.

3. Bend the elbows. The elbow should usually form an obtuse angle (greater then 90 degrees). With a lesser angle, the bridge loses structural integrity and can be collapsed by an opponent. The angle should not be so great, however, that the arm begins to straighten. A straight arm can be slipped under or around, and can be more easily jammed and locked. Even with motions like the thrusting punch or darting fingers, the arms extend for only the instant in which power is applied, relaxing and naturally bending again immediately thereafter.

4. Center the wrists. The wrists tend to maintain a position along the meridian line. As with the elbow, this is both the simplest and most direct route to the opponent and allows the body's full structure to be behind the hand. Oftentimes, the fingers will also be placed on the mutual meridian line, pointing intently toward the opponent. This serves to both create a threatening presence (like a snake about to strike) and to ensure proper dominance of the position.

PART THREE

拳套路

Forms

CHAPTER 5

The Opening Form

The *hoi sik* (opening form) is a unique and distinctive sequence that is performed at the beginning of all Yuen Kay-San wing chun kuen routines. The opening form is composed of a short series of basic movements. All of the motions in the opening form are also found later in other routines, however their early introduction is thought to be beneficial in the training of new practitioners.

The opening form has evolved over the generations. The forms of Fok Bo-Chuen were said to have begun with an opening sequence very similar to the palm-down rising of the arms seen in other branches and arts. Yuen Kay-San, wanting something more distinctive for his branch, made some modifications and later asked Sum Nung to choreograph a new opening. Under Yuen's supervision, Sum Nung formalized the sequence still used today to identify the wing chun kuen descending from Yuen Kay-San and Sum Nung.

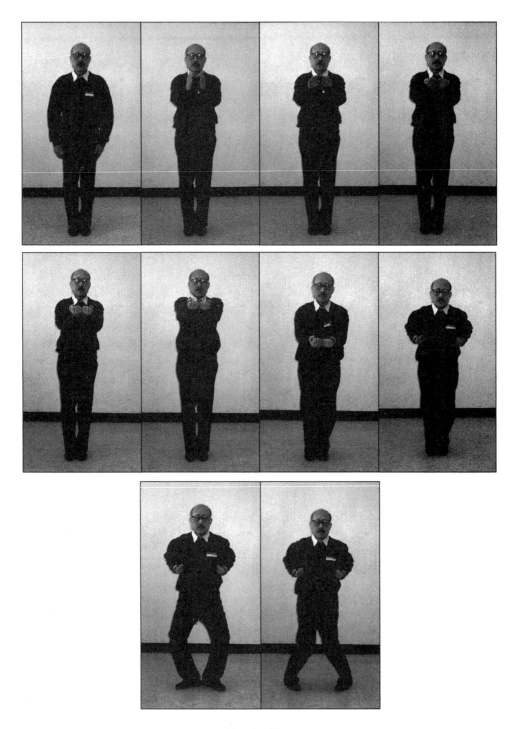

Opening Form

1. Starting position. Forms begin with the feet together, arms down by their sides, and the body and mind relaxed and centered.

2. Raise the arms up. The elbows remain in and bend naturally until the tips of the fingers reach shoulder height. The fingers are held gently together and the palms face inward.

3. Turn the wrists out. The wrists snap out, turning the palms downward.

4. Rotate the hands. Keeping the elbows in place, the wrists rotate, turning the hands over until the palms face upward.

5. Close the fists. The fists are closed one set of knuckles at a time with the thumbs placed over the index fingers.

6. Extend the arms. This motion requires the elbows to come together and move the arms along the meridian line until they are almost completely straight, fists level with the shoulders.

7. Drop the arms and posture. The elbows sink downward and in next to the ribs while the hands drop down, staying on the meridian line as long as possible, until the wrists assume a position just below the elbows. At the same time, the knees bend, sinking the posture down.

8. Retract the arms and sink the posture. The hands rise up as the elbows ram backward, withdrawing the fists at chest level with the backs of the hands facing down. The sinking of the posture concludes at the same moment.

9. Rotate the toes out. The feet rotate on the heels until the toes point outward.

10. Rotate the heels out. The feet then rotate on the front of the foot until the heels point outward.

The initial movements of the opening form represent *dap kiu* (joining bridges). This is the elemental embodiment of the joining concept. At its most basic level, the joining bridge trains the practitioner to raise the arms from a relaxed, unprepared posture to a position capable of defense and offense. This is important because one never knows when or from where an attack may come and the body needs to be able to reflexively assume simple intercepting structures. Although the actual position itself can be used in application, it is better thought of as an example of the concept since the bridges can be joined using many different structural formations.

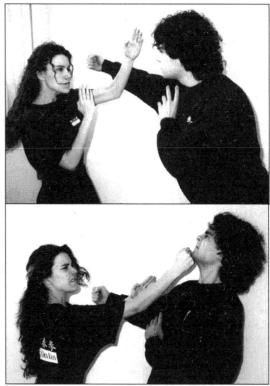

Antony suddenly launches a surprise attack at Georgia from the side. Seeing it out of her peripheral vision, she quickly raises a joining arm to establish contact and then counters with a thrusting punch.

The outward rotation of the wrists helps to develop penetrating inch-power in the outside fore-arm and can be seen as the first example of *lan sao*. The term *lan* means to "bar, block, or obstruct passage," thus the barring arm is used to obstruct the passage of an opponent or their limbs. Like all points, it is conceptual and thus there are several different structural formations used for the barring arm. The variation used here is also found in the Yuen Kay-San wooden dummy form. Its inclusion in the opening form, and in one of the first san sao drills, reflects its usefulness in early application training.

Lan sao chung choi (barring arm thrusting punch) utilizes the barring arm from the opening form with a simultaneous thrusting punch and the 45-degree side horse. It illustrates a two armed version of "linked defense with offense," trains the arms to function independently, and helps build inch power. Alternating can be accomplished by either directly changing the arms from one to the other (barring to punch or vice versa) or by relaxing and dropping the arms between repetitions. The former better trains quick changing to engage multiple swinging attacks while the latter helps to build the reflexes needed to swiftly move from a natural to engaged condition.

Ngo sifu demonstrates the barring arm thrusting punch, among the first san sao learned in the system. In application, when Antony swings towards her temple, Georgia simultaneously strikes Antony's punch with the barring arm while countering down the median line with the thrusting punch. Antony manages to get another swing off, but Georgia simply changes to bar and strike again.

The small *gwa* (hanging), backfist-like motion can be found here in the turning over of the palm and also in the transition of many other movements. In this capacity, it can serve to quickly change the arm from underneath to above the opponent's bridge, or to strike swiftly (usually using a fist) when the opportunity presents itself.

Closing the hand one knuckle at a time helps to form a relaxed, yet solid fist. Not tense, yet without "space" inside. Although essentially basic training, *jia kuen* (closing fist) can build reflexes that can be used both defensively (closing the fist to avoid a joint-locking attempt directed at the fingers) and offensively (to form a fist quickly when striking).

Closing the elbows, as noted in the previous chapter, is an important concept in wing chun kuen. In times past, it was said that wing chun kuen practitioners who began training at a very young age would use small wooden rings, placed around their elbows, to develop this skill. As they grew older, continued use of the ring would help them retain the flexibility to keep the elbows in. The movement of the arms on the meridian line with both the wrists and elbows touching is another way to develop the flexibility and relaxation needed for this essential element.

Both the dropping of the arms and backward retraction of the elbows merge to form the *sao kuen* (ending fists), but also serve to reinforce cardinal principles. The first part of this movement can be seen as a type of sinking elbow saving arm (as seen in the *siu lien tao* and other forms). Following the principle of no wasted movement, the withdrawing action of the arms is done with as much intention as any other motion. This helps in the training of both direct backward techniques such as *da pao jaan* (wrapping hitting elbow), as well as the development of the power later used in pulling. It also works to improve the flexibility of the shoulders, which will help them remain relaxed.

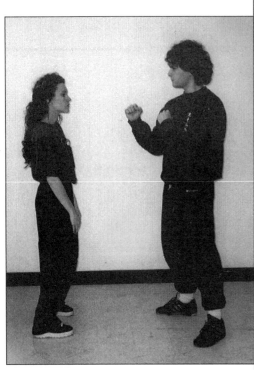

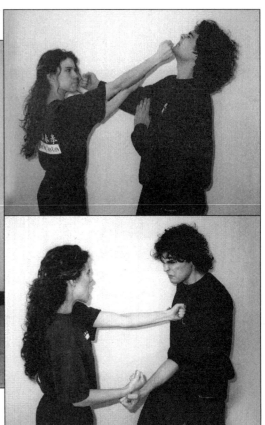

While countering Antony's attack, Georgia exposes her ribs. Antony tries to take advantage of the opening with a follow up punch but Georgia reflexively closes them off with a sinking elbow saving arm and strikes with her other fist.

Georgia walks, unsuspecting, as Rene approaches from the rear. When Rene moves to grab her, Georgia, feeling his arms closing about her, slices her front arm forward to disrupt his grab while at the same time slamming her elbow backward.

The posture taken in the opening form is the *yee jee kim yeung ma* (trapezoid-shaped clamping groin horse, also referred to as trapezoid-shaped clamping goat horse). *Yee jee* refers to the "shape of the Chinese character *yee*," in this sense a trapezoid with the top line slightly smaller then the bottom, just as the knees are clamped in closer then the width of the feet. *Kim yeung* means to clamp, protecting the groin. The alternate rendering, which sounds identical, can be translated to mean, "clamping goat," in reference to the old practice of restraining a goat between the knees.

Antony is talking to Georgia when she suddenly flicks a kick at his groin. Antony immediately sinks his posture and clamps his knees to ward it off. As she is about to place her foot back down, Antony slices in and strikes.

The fundamental horse of the style, trapezoid-shaped clamping groin horse teaches the body to assume a naturally balanced and aligned position that can easily transfer power between the ground and the opponent. A structurally sound, pyramid-like platform that enables the use of both sides of the body equally, at its most basic level it can also protect the groin from an upward swinging attack.

The trapezoid shaped clamping groin horse also forms the basis of the *bai jong* (assume posture), or the neutral pre-engagement, ready position of the system. The old version of the ready posture usually consisted of the trapezoid shaped clamping groin horse in conjunction with a joining bridge and guarding arm. Grandmaster Sum Nung reportedly felt that this posture telegraphed too much aggressive intent and gave away too many characteristics of the practitioner's martial art system. Thus, just as one wouldn't stand holding out a dispersing arm in case someone threw a punch toward it, it was thought one shouldn't assume a rigid horse in application until the moment it is needed. The latter ready posture favors a natural horse that can quickly change into the trapezoid-shaped clamping groin horse, side horse, moving horse, or any combination thereof as needed. Likewise, the hands are left relaxed until an opponent approaches close enough to be considered an imminent threat. At that point, one arm can inquire their intentions and the other guard, also as needed. It is from the ready posture that many of the *san sao* drills begin.

CHAPTER 6

The 12 Forms

The *sup yee sik* (12 forms), sometimes referred to as the *sup yee san sao* (12 separate techniques), descend from the teachings of Cheung Bo and were integrated into Yuen Kay-San wing chun kuen by grandmaster Sum Nung.

The wing chun kuen of Cheung Bo did not make use of any forms, but consisted solely of *san sao*. In terms of structure, Cheung Bo's large, muscular build made it difficult for him to keep his elbows closed on the meridian line (as was the practice of Yuen Kay-San and some other wing chun boxers of the time). Thus, Cheung used wider arms and compensated with quick and powerful side-body horse changes.

When teaching in Guangzhou, grandmaster Sum Nung used some of the techniques as early training for his students, developing in them a powerful foundation. The remaining forms came later, serving as complementary exercises. Although the methods of Yuen Kay-San refined the *sup yee sik* to a great extent, a few still retain their characteristic wide detaining arms and defensive shifts, while some seem to possess hybrid qualities of both approaches. Grandmaster Sum Nung also integrated some of the movements from the *sup yee sik* into the beginning sections of the Yuen Kay-San wooden dummy form.

Compact in structure, yet containing many of the elements essential to a good wing chun kuen foundation, the *sup yee sik* are ideal for early training. The first four focus on building body structure through basic punching, turning, and stepping drills. The next four work fundamental arm cycles, firmly ingraining the cardinal tools for interception and changing the bridges. The last four include sensitivity training and combination techniques.

It should be noted that there are sometimes variations among the *sup yee sik* from branch to branch in the Yuen Kay-San system. Sometimes the order differs, sometimes the names are slightly different, and sometimes different techniques are used in the sequence, such as the double circling arms in place of the sticking single bridge. In the lines descending from Kwok Jin-Fen (an early student of grandmaster Sum Nung), elements of the *sup yee sik* are often taught as two choreographed sets. The first four forms are combined into a linking set called *sei go gen ben choi* (four basic punches). The *lien wan gaun kao sao* (linked chain cultivating and detaining arms) then combines the flapping wing palms with other techniques such as the phoenix-eye punch, barring arm thrusting punch, wing arm grasping strike, and so on. It is also said that Yuen Kay-San knew very similar techniques and worked on their refinement.

The *sup yee sik* include: 1) meridian punch; 2) side punch; 3) single dragon punch; 4) arrow punch; 5) triangle palm; 6) inside outside yin and yang palm; 7) inside join; 8) outside join; 9) detaining joining arm; 10) flapping wing palms; 11) single sticking bridge; and 12) white crane seizes the fox.

Meridian Punch

子午鎚

The *jee ng choi* (meridian punch) trains wing chun kuen body structure through the fundamental trapezoid-shaped clamping groin horse and the primary thrusting punch of the style, which pounds explosively along the meridian line. Its extensions include the concussive linked chain punches and the three star punches. The meridian punch also teaches alignment on the meridian line, attacking the opponent's meridian line, and the domination of the mutual meridian line. In short, the principles behind wing chun kuen's straight body methods.

Meridian punch

1. Open the form.

2. Align the fist. From its retracted position, the left fist moves onto the meridian line while the elbow stays in against the body.

3. Extend the punch. Continuing the motion, the elbow comes onto the meridian line, helping drive the fist forward. As it reaches extension, the back of the hand should be facing outward. Power is only emitted in the final instant of extension and the arm is relaxed again immediately thereafter.

4. Drop the arm and align the next fist. When alternating, the dropping of the left arm (as described in the opening form) should end roughly as the fist of the right punch is coming onto the meridian line.

5. Withdraw the arm and extend the next punch. Likewise, the left elbow should explode backward in the same instant the right punch thrusts forward.

Following the opening form, the meridian punch is usually the first technique learned in wing chun kuen and many of the cardinal "seeds" of the system can be found within. Some systems advocate the independent training of the horse, usually by "sitting" in them for long periods. Wing chun kuen, however, in keeping with the economical nature of the style, considers it sensible to also drill the upper body while the lower body is being trained.

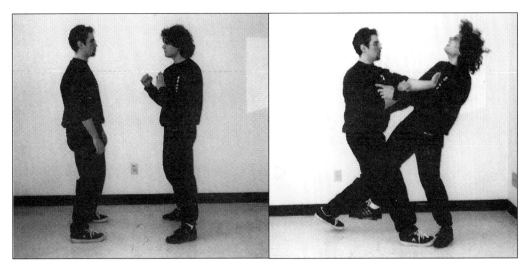

Rene, seeing Antony about to trust out a punch, reacts by sinking and slicing his meridiaN punch through Antony's bridge and into his center. This controls his opponent's arm, breaks his structure, and counters at the same time.

The meridian punch employs a *yat jee chung choi* (vertical-shaped thrusting punch). Yat jee refers to "the shape of the Chinese character *yat.*" This character takes the form of a vertical rectangle bisected horizontally and represents in this context the fist held vertically, thumb side up. The initial alignment of the fist on the meridian line helps ensure that the punch dominates that line from the beginning and travels in a straight path throughout, lowering its visible profile and providing the fastest route possible to the opponent.

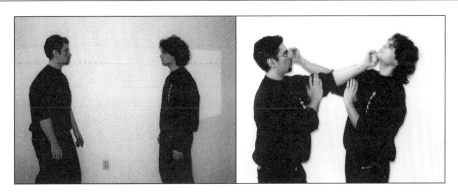

This time, when Antony strikes, Rene's meridian punch rises and slices from the inside, dispersing Antony's attack and simultaneously striking him.

There are two main methods used in aligning the fist. The first keeps the fist with the back of the hand facing down and turns it to the vertical position during extension. This can aid in applying spiraling power and in suppressing an opponent's bridge while punching. The second method aligns the fist immediately in the vertical position and extends it from there. This can provide a stronger structure for issuing straight force and cleaving through obstructions.

The punch itself does not scoop upward nor swing downward, but rather flies straight forward along the meridian line at shoulder height (the neutral position for training) like an arrow being launched from a powerful bow. The beginning and the end of wing chun kuen, this technique is perhaps its most refined expression. Illustrating wing chun kuen's straight body methods, it embodies the single limb concept of "linked defense and attack," as the arm's domination of the meridian line can intercept and control an opponent's bridge while the fist strikes.

Punches can be alternated as much as desired for training purposes. Drilling of the punch can be accomplished with several different types of equipment.

Da yeung juk (candle hitting) works to train the focus of the meridian punch. The candle should be set up so that the flame is at shoulder height, aligned with the punch. Beginning a short distance from the candle, punches are performed and the direction in which the flame moves can help guide the focus of power. Clean power should travel straight without the fist shaking or vibrating at the end, and should move the flame distinctly backward in line with the punch (as opposed to just jostling it around in random directions). Although the drill can also be done with the intention of extinguishing the wick, it is preferable to increase the distance from the candle to keep this as difficult as possible.

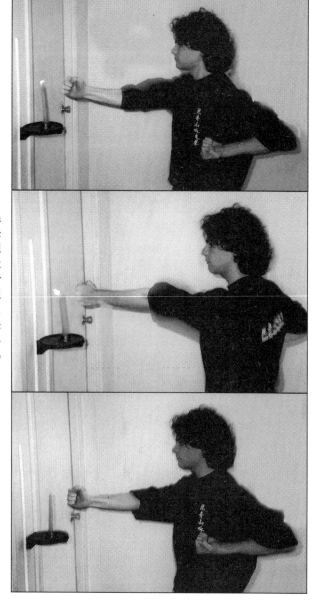

The candle punching exercise allows Antony to watch the direction of the flame's movement, helping develope the clarity and focus of the meridian punch.

Da sa bao (sandbag hitting) training is useful for developing the structure of the punch. The sandbag is usually composed of a square canvas bag filled with sand, dried beans, small stones, iron shot, or other substance suitable to the practitioners training level. Sandbags can be placed at various heights to train flexible punching. It is important to begin slowly and train in a progressive manner. The striking surface of the punch in the drill and in application, is the entire front of the fist, using primarily the middle two knuckles whose direct alignment with the elbow provides solid structure for the technique. The exact location can vary, however, depending on the direction at which the punch is angled (if any), and the nature of the target being struck.

Antony trains the structured power of the meridian punch on the sandbags.

Muk yan jong (wooden dummy) is perhaps the most famous of the wing chun kuen training aids. It is constructed to match the size of its intended user and is composed of a body post, two high-level arms, a single mid-level arm, and a low-level leg. When originally developed, the dummy was buried quite deeply in the ground and surrounded by loose earth. As apartments grew more common, this arrangement became impractical, if not impossible (especially if one lived above ground level), so the wooden dummy was redesigned to incorporate a solid metal base with heavy-duty springs. Although a set form is taught at more advanced levels, a wing chun kuen practitioner can use the wooden dummy right from the beginning to train almost any motion. Drilling on the wooden dummy helps to develop the bridges and body structure, build precision and accuracy in movements, and aids in the development of short-range, explosive energy.

The withdrawal of the first strike is identical in form to those found in the opening sequence. During the meridian punch, however, it also serves to clear the path for the next strike, allowing it to travel straight down the meridian line. It is important that the withdrawal is performed with the same speed and power as the meridian punch itself. Following the nature of yum yeung, as one bridge goes out, the other comes back; as one hand pushes out, the other draws in. The two motions and powers balance each other.

The meridian punch and other punching drills are also sometimes practiced with the hand withdrawing upwards instead of downwards, clearing an under the bridge path for the next strike.

Linked Chain Punch

Lien wan choi (linked chain punch) extends the concepts found in the meridian punch and is very similar in foundation. The major difference lies in the fact that the arm, upon completion of the punch, withdraws back only so far as the elbow.

 The linked chain punch is the practical application of the meridian punch. It allows a practitioner to launch strikes (or other techniques) quickly and overwhelmingly. When in use, it is not economical (or even sensible) to re-chamber an arm after every technique. Rather, it is preferable to withdraw them only slightly, assuming a guarding position from which other techniques can quickly follow. The withdrawing motion in the linked chain punch itself can be quite functional, serving to suppress the bridges of an opponent in order to keep the path clear for the next punch or technique.

The linked chain punch can be trained with the candle, sandbag, and wooden dummy in the same manner as the meridian punch proper.

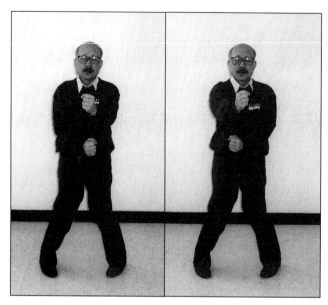

Linked Chain Punch

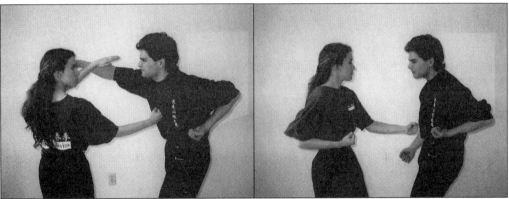

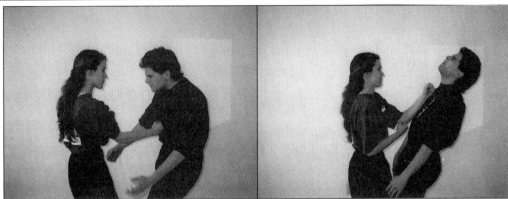

When Antony attacks, Georgia counters with a barring arm thrusting punch. With Antony momentarily interrupted, Georgia quickly follows up with linked chain punches to end the encounter.

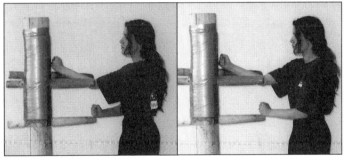

The linked chain punch can also be practiced on the sandbags and the wooden dummy.

Side Punch

Pien choi (side punch), also known as *pien san choi* (side body punch) adds side horse turning to the thrusting punch, and works on developing the connected power of the body. The side punch also trains the facing posture, side body, and flanking methods of wing chun kuen. Its extensions include the kneeling side punch.

Side Punch

1. Open the form.

2. Align the fist, turn, and punch. The fist aligns as described in the meridian punch. As the left punch extends, the body turns 90 degrees to the right so that the hips and shoulders both face to the side.

3. Alternate. Using the same method outlined in the meridian punch, as the body turns back toward center, one arm drops and the other aligns. Continuing smoothly, the body turns to the left as the right punch extends and the left withdraws.

Practicing the side punch is one of the most important basic drills of the system. As a youth in Foshan, grandmaster Sum Nung drilled the technique so much that he wore ditches in the tiles on which he trained.

Georgia and Rene stand facing each other with bridges joined on the meridian line. When Rene pressed forward to punch, Georgia shifts to the side and counters. In this position, Georgia remains locked on the meridian line while Rene's bridges point off harmlessly to the side. As Rene attempts to regain positioning, Georgia changes and shifting again, maintains dominance of the mutual meridian.

The side punch builds on the foundation of the meridian punch. The basic punching motion is the same and all of the structural guidelines given for the lower body apply to the pien ma (side horse). It differs from the trapezoid- shaped clamping groin horse in that as the hips turn, the vast majority of the body's weight shifts onto one leg (in this case the leg on the same side of the body as the punching arm). When turning, the head stays looking straight forward and the knees remain clamped.

Connected power in wing chun kuen involves the horse, waist, and arms working together. All three begin and end their motion at the same time. The training of the side punch is one of the earliest and most important tools for the development of this concept.

The side punch has many uses in application. It can be used to align with a turning opponent (following the principle of "facing body") or to close off the opponent's center while leaving the practitioner's own center "locked on" (illustrating wing chun kuen's flanking method). It can also be employed to accompany a retreating opponent (encapsulating the principle of "chasing form") or to add power to bridges going out or coming in. Additionally, the side punch can be used to move the upper body quickly off the meridian and to swiftly empty the weight off one leg (to ward against lower body attacks/manipulations or ready an offensive technique).

In training, the side horse turns a full 90 degrees to ensure maximum range of motion. In application, however, practitioners should only turn the minimum amount necessary to achieve their objective. Drills for the side punch employ several two-person exercises.

In one drill, two partners stand in close proximity while practicing the side punch. Both partners execute the punch at the same time, with the same arm (right and right, left and left), each following the posture of the other. This helps ensure that both practitioners fully remove their torso's from the meridian line.

Lai yiu (pulling waist) is also fundamental training for the side horse. Practitioners stand facing each other with matching grasping arms (right on right or vice versa). One partner uses the connected power of the horse to turn sideways, changing the grasping arm into a pressing arm as the other partner is directed off the line. Learning to root, to use the body for power, and to "sit" in the stance are all part of the pulling waist exercise.

As more tools are learned, the waist pulling exercise is broadened to include things such as elbow and shoulder attacks and controls, horse disruption and recovery methods, and other elements.

Antony and Rene practice face-to-face punching. This drill helps develop the concept of facing posture and of changing the meridian line.

Antony and Rene face each other with matching grasping arms for the waist pulling exercise. Taking turns, Antony utilizes connected body power to displace Rene, after which they return to the neutral position and Rene performs the drill.

Kneeling Side Punch

跪
地
偏
錘

Gwai dei pien choi (kneeling side punch), sometimes called *gwai ma choi* (kneeling horse punch), drops the knee straight down, rapidly lowering the body during the turning motion. As in the side punch, the body works in unity, with the knee beginning its drop as the punch and turn begin and ending as the punch and turn end. It is typically drilled by alternating one standard side punch with one kneeling side punch. This provides good training for the legs and helps to develop dynamic changing ability from high- to low-level techniques.

Kneeling side punch

The kneeling side punch can be used for both defense and offense very close to the ground level.

When asked about the practicality of the kneeling side punch, grandmaster Sum Nung once told a story about Yuen Kay-San's friend, Yip Man, using the technique to win a fight. A man had launched a powerful low footsweep at Yip, who quickly dropped into the kneeling side punch, efficiently barring the sweep and countering at the same time.

When Rene steps forward with a swinging attack, Antony employs a side kneeling punch to drop below the attack and counter.

As Rene drops to attack with a low sweeping kick, Antony uses the side kneeling punch to obstruct the attack and damage his opponent's leg while countering with a thrusting punch.

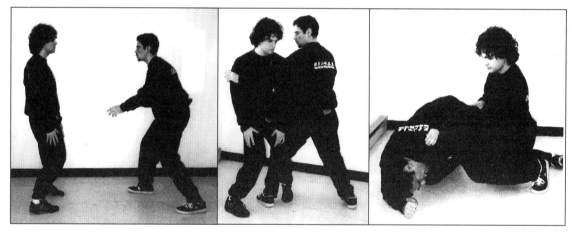

Antony remains rooted in his clamping horse when Rene shoots in and tries to sweep him. When Rene's attack falters, Antony counters by breaking Rene's stance with the kneeling horse and simultaneously seizing and controlling his arm with a butterfly palm maneuver.

Single Dragon Punch

獨
龍
錘

Duk lung choi (single dragon punch) combines elements of the previous forms, training them in a complementary manner. It alternates a side projecting punch from the front horse and a front projecting punch from the side horse. It also integrates the linked chain punch and introduces the fundamental wing arm movement. In addition, like the chum kiu form, the single dragon punch helps train the reflexes to intercept and counter attacks from the side and back, completing the four directions of basic training.

1. Open the form.

2. Extend the punch. From its chambered position, the left fist travels along the side meridian, with the elbow driving behind.

3. Turn and extend the forward punch. The body turns 90 degrees to the left while the left punch withdraws and the right punch aligns to and then extends along the meridian line.

4. Turn and alternate. The body turns back to the front while the right punch withdraws and the left punch extends along the side meridian. Steps three and four may be repeated as often as desired during training before changing direction (steps five and six).

5. Chain punch. During a repetition of step three, linked chain punches are executed to begin the direction change. Any odd number of punches may be used. On the last punch, the right arm should be extended and the left arm re-chambered completely.

6. Turn and sweep the arm. The body turns a full 180 degrees until the hips and shoulders squarely face the left. Simultaneously, the right arm cuts downward before sweeping upward. In its final position, the fingers point forward, the wrist aligns vertically at nose level, and the elbow is slightly higher then the wrist.

7. Extend the forward punch. The right arm drops down and withdraws as the left arm punches.

8. Turn and alternate. The body turns and the next punch is executed. As before, these punches may be alternated as often as desired before changing sides again.

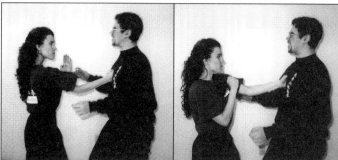

Georgia stands calmly while Rene approaches from the side. As he moves to strike, Georgia moves first, launching a punch to the side. The attack disrupted, Georgia immediately turns to face her attacker and follows up with linked chain punches.

The name "single dragon punch" retains the old tradition of poetic names for movements. These served to inspire practitioners and to disguise the meaning of movements to outsiders. Over time, however, many of these old names have been replaced using more technically oriented terminology. The single dragon punch is one of several that are still preserved in the Yuen Kay-San system.

Since the sideways punch originates from the side meridian (as opposed to the meridian line utilized in the previous two forms), the fist is already roughly in position and does not require aligning. The head should turn to the side, following the direction of the punches. This motion helps train the practitioner to reflexively react to attacks approaching from the side when there may not be enough time to turn and intercept them in the usual front-body manner.

The turning punch can also be used to deal with attacks from the side when slightly more reaction time is available. In addition, due to its method of execution and the power it generates, it can be devastating as a follow-up maneuver.

The next two motions are introduced here in order to give one an idea of the concepts needed when an opponent attacks from behind.

The sweeping of the arm during the changing of sides can be seen as an example of a joining bridge used to determine the nature of an attack approaching from behind while the body is turning to face it. Sweeping ensures a large area is covered in case the exact position of an incoming strike can not be immediately determined. If something is encountered during the sweep, the arm can quickly contact it and change to an appropriate response.

Rene comes up behind Georgia, preparing a sneak attack. Seeing a potentially dangerous
movement, Georgia turns and utilizes a wing arm to sweep the area and join with any incoming bridges.
Rene, his initial attack thwarted, tries to follow up with a quick jab at Georgia's exposed ribs. Georgia intercepts with a saving arm and counters with a thrusting punch.

The position assumed following the turn is a version of the high bong sao (wing arm). The word
bong represents the "side limit of the body," often translated as "wing" or "shoulder." The
immediate change from the wing arm to the withdrawal is an early example of the saying "a
wing arm does not stop or stay." A wing arm exists only long enough to disperse an attack or
disrupt an attacker and then instantly changes into a counter or another arm structure.

Arrow Punch

Jin choi (arrow punch) adds basic linear stepping to the striking work begun in the
meridian punch and the turning work of the side punch and single dragon punch. It
also trains the lower body in both defense (quick rooting, changing the meridian line,
etc.) and offense (striking, uprooting, controlling, etc.).

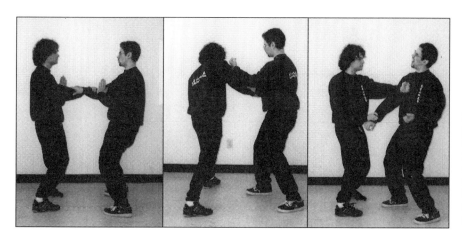

From the double grasping arm position, Rene gives Antony a sudden pull. Antony, however, uses a side step to change the line and counters with a detaining arm and thrusting punch.

In form, the arrow punch is identical to the single dragon punch. During the alternating of punches, however, a step is performed in the same direction as the punch is travelling. A side step during the side punch, an arrow step during the front punch. Stepping is no exception to the principles of connected power and like every other element it begins and ends at the same time as the turn and punch. The mechanics consist of lifting the front foot, allowing the stored power of pressed knees to begin the movement, and the drive of the back leg to continue it. As the front foot touches down, the clamping action of the knees pulls the back foot into position again. The turn is completed.

Rene lunges forward with an attack and Antony directs him off to the side, overextending him. Antony then slices into his center with an arrow horse, scooping him up and throwing him off with butterfly palms.

Both the arrow step and the side step can be used to quickly root following a movement, as tools to stick to or to lock the opponent's lower extremities, as offensive weapons for striking an opponent with the lower body, or for slicing into them to destroy their structure.

As Antony begins a jumping spinning kick, Georgia immediately moves forward with the arrow step. Once inside Antony's attack, Georgia disrupts the kick and sends him falling to the floor, hard.

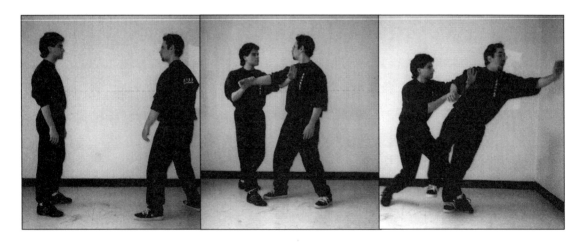

When Rene attacks, Antony grasps his bridge, steps forward and controls both Rene's legs with an arrow horse. This destroys Rene's stability and sends him tumbling.

Triangle Palms

Sam pan jeung (triangle palms) drills a simple set of three arm movements that cover basic changes and interceptions outside, inside, and downward. The name of this set can be seen as representing the triangle described by the three movements and of the triangular nature of wing chun kuen wedging in general.

Triangle Palms

1 Open the form.

2. Extend the arm. The left arm moves out along the meridian line. The palm faces up and slants to the side while the fingers slope slightly downward.

3. Push the palm. The left elbow retracts slightly before the palm pushes sideways, aligning with the shoulder of the right arm

4. Chop the arm downwards. The left bridge cuts downward until the wrist is on the meridian line with the elbow bent and the palm facing in at dan tian height.

5. Alternate. Alternating can be accomplished by the arm rising up again to renew the cycle or by the left arm withdrawing and the right extending.

The triangle palms set is usually matched in application with a partner performing three punches. The first two are done at shoulder level, the third lower. This helps the practitioner become familiar with varying the placement of movements in quick succession.

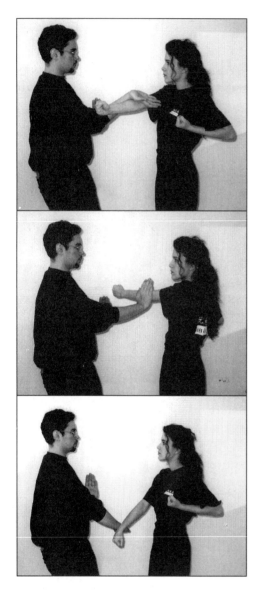

The first motion represents a type of *tan sao* (dispersing arm) identical to that found in the *siu lien tao* form's "three prayers to Buddha" section. *Tan* is often mistranslated as "palm up" but in actuality represents "spreading out" or "dispersing." In this sense, it disperses an opponent's force, not allowing it to be absorbed by the practitioner's body and can spread out the opponent's limbs, creating openings for counters. Travelling from under to over, inside to outside, the dispersing arm is one of the principle intercepting tools of wing chun kuen. The structure of the hand helps increase sensitivity and properly channel and dissipate an opponent's force away from the body. The position of the elbow and wrist on the meridian line is ideal for outside interception (right intercepting right or left intercepting left). When intercepting on the inside, the elbow and wrist can align just inside shoulder width instead.

The pushing movement illustrates *chang jeung* (supporting palm) similar to both versions found later in the siu lien tao form. The supporting palm does not shock an opponent's bridge like the slapping arm seen in later forms, but rather establishes contact and redirects the attacking limb. Swallowing rather than opposing the opponent's force makes the technique more difficult to detect and leak through.

The downward chopping of the arm forms the *gaun sao* (cultivating arm) that can be employed to protect the lower area of the body. Depending on how it is used, the cultivating arm can either blend with and redirect force or cut into it and injure the attacking limb.

In a standard drill, Rene employs the dispersing arm, supporting palm, and cultivating arm to intercept Georgia's linked high and low punch.

Tan huen (rattan ring) training helps to develop the splitting power of bridges such as the cultivating arm. The ring varies in size depending on the user but should fit comfortably around the bridges when placed in position.

Antony trains the splitting power of the dispersing arm and cultivating arm with a variation of the rattan ring.

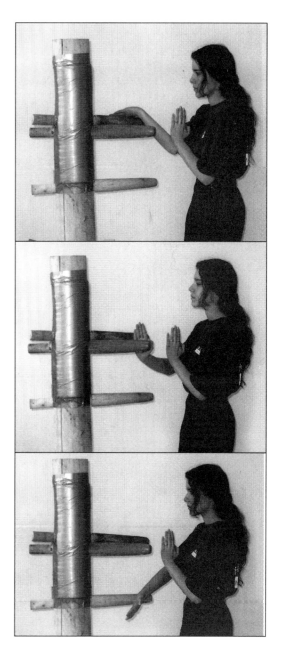

The wooden dummy can also be used to train the structure of the triangle palms.

In application, Rene uses the dispersing hit to channel Antony 's attack away from his center, a supporting palm to control Antony's elbow and close him off the center, and a cultivating arm to ward off a low attack.

Inside Outside Yin and Yang Palms

里
廉
陰
陽
掌

Loi lim yum yeung jeung (inside outside *yin* and *yang* palms), also known by the more common name of *tan fook sao* (dispersing and controlling arms), develops two of the primary wing chun kuen intercepting tools in a short but densely packed set. It also teaches the yin and yang and "one long, one short" concepts behind smoothly changing the bridges.

1. Open the form.

2. Position the arms. The left arm extends forward in line roughly with the shoul der and assumes a dispersing arm posi tion. The right hand takes position roughly below the elbow of the left arm, with the palm facing down.

3. Alternate. In a smooth cycle, the left arm folds down while the right arm weaves the palm upward into the extended position.

The relative position of the dispersing arm at shoulder width enhances its usefulness in inside-the-body application (right intercepting left or vice versa). When used on the outside, it should align on the meridian line as described in the triangle palm set.

Inside Outside Yin and Yang Palms

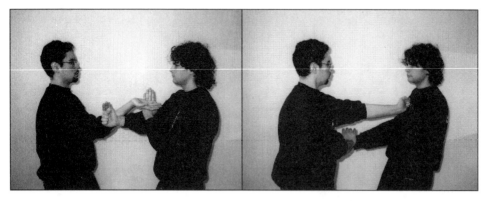

During the practice of the dispersing arm, Rene employs a folding controlling arm and thrusting punch.

The folding arm is a type of *fook sao* (controlling arm). The character for *fook* means to "control" or "subdue" and represents a person (in this case the practitioner's arm) taming a dog (the opponent's arm). As mentioned previously, wing chun kuen's conceptual nature means that it sometimes has different physical shapes for the same core motion. Thus, while the controlling arm introduced in this set is different in appearance from that found in the inside or outside join sets or the *siu lien tao* form, it remains identical in principle.

Ngo sifu demonstrates the half-wing-half-dispersing movement. In application, when Rene attacks, Georgia guides him down and to the side with the half-wing-half-dispersing technique before following up with hanging punch to the solar-plexus and drilling punch to the throat.

This version works well to quickly subdue an arm that has come inside the bridge and to control more then one bridge at the same time. Depending on the situation, the folding arm can also take on characteristics of the *pak sao* (slapping arm).

Georgia attacks Rene with a round-house kick. Rene charges the center while joining with the half-dispersing-half-wing bridge. As her leg begins to come down, Rene strikes with his shoulder, sending her crashing to the floor.

Aside from the basic dispersing arm and folding controlling arm, the yin and yang palm can also be extended into the boon tan bong (half dispersing, half wing), the jao sao (running arm), and others.

Georgia trains the yin and yang palms and the half-wing-half-dispersing on the wooden dummy.

Inside Join

Noi dap (inside join) also sometimes referred to as noi lim sao (inside sickle arm) is the first of two related sets and cycles a basic interior controlling arm movement with an outside circling arm. The inside join trains the reflexive closing of the meridian line and the changing of positions from the inside to the outside. Its extensions include the inside grasp.

1. Open the form.

2. Position the arms and turn. The left arm extends outward until the elbow is on the meridian line with the palm facing downward and the fingers pointing forward. The right hand simultaneously circles downward to the meridian line at a point just below the elbow of the left arm. At the same time, the body rotates right, in a 45-degree version of the side horse, moving the arms inside.

3. Alternate. In a smooth cycle the right arm rises and the left arm drops, swapping positions. Simultaneously, the body turns to face 45 degrees left of center.

Inside Join

The high arm represents another form of controlling arm (this one similar to the version used to control the wing arm during luk sao practice). Since one never knows where an attack may come from, this movement helps train the reflexes to close and control the meridian line from an outside to inside position.

While Georgia is speaking, Antony tries to steal a strike at her exposed center. Georgia closes off the attack with an inside join and quickly moves to detain his bridge and counter.

The lower arm can function as a *huen sao* (circling arm) or *kao sao* (detaining arm) used to clear the meridian line or to change positions (from inside to outside or vice versa).

Inside Grasp

The *noi lop* (inside grasp) is an extension of the inside join that follows with *lop sao* (grasping arm) in application to maintain control of an opponent's bridge.

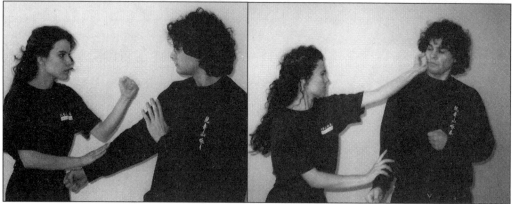

Antony thrusts his fist forward and Georgia makes contact
She then uses an inside grasping hand to change to the outside while countering.

Inside join training on the wooden dummy.

Outside Join

外
搭

Ngoi dap (outside join), also sometimes referred to as *ngoi lim sao* (outside sickle arm) is the complement of the inside join, combining a basic exterior controlling arm movement with the inside circling arm. The outside grasp is an extension of the outside join.

Outside Join

1 Open the form.

2. Position the arms and turn. The arms are positioned identically to the inside join. The turn, however, is performed in the opposite direction. This brings the extended arm from inside out and the lower arm from outside in, respectively.

3. Alternate. The arms alternate in the same manner as the inside join. Again, only the direction of the horse change differs.

As would be expected, the functions of the movements of the outside join are the same as those of the inside join, differing only in their direction. This controlling arm clears the body from the inside out, while the circling arm moves from the outside in.

Antony is distracted while facing Georgia. When Georgia throws a punch at him, Antony employs an outside join to close himself off before detaining her bridge and countering.

Antony counters Georgia's swing and uses the outside join to change to the outside and follows up with a cultivating arm strike.

The outside join being practiced on the wooden dummy.

外擺

Outside Grasp

The *ngoi lop* (outside grasp) is an extension of outside join. It utilizes a grasping arm in application to control an opponent's bridge.

Linked asking arms is a sticking drill that involves the changes from outside to inside and vice versa. It can be performed with either the detaining arm or grasping arm. In the drill, one partner alternates punches while the other intercepts and controls with one arm while countering with the other. The countering arm is left extended on the meridian line, inquiring into the opponent's next move. The attacking partner can answer by striking again on either the inside or outside of the inquiring arm. If the attack is on the outside, an outside detain or grasp will intercept. On the inside, an inside detain or grasp wil intercept. In either case, the counter is again left out, inquiring. The process continues until the partners switch roles. This exercise helps develop the smooth changing of the arms, the sensitivity of the bridges, swallowing rather then opposing force, and the concept of "asking the way."

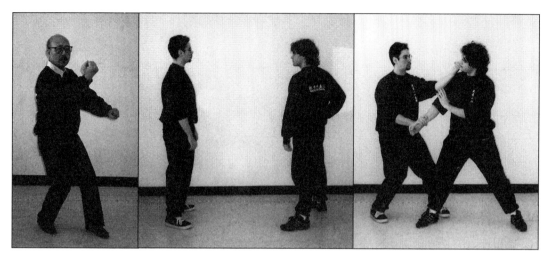

Ngo sifu demonstrates the grasping arm hanging punch. In application, Rene intercepts and controls Antony's lunging punch with the grasping arm while covering and countering with the hanging punch.

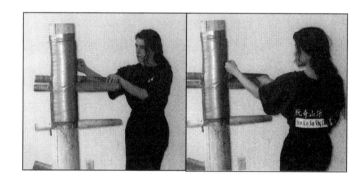

Georgia practices the outside grasp and punch on the wooden dummy.

Detaining Joining Arms

扣
搭
手

Kao dap sao (detaining joining arms) utilizes a Cheung Bo style wide detaining arm along with a hanging punch and suffocating structure. It trains the practitioner to deal with heavy chain attacks, keep the flank, and to break an opponent's center.

1. Open the form.

2. Fold the bridge and turn. The right arm folds downward as the body begins to turn right.

3. Hook upward and punch. The right arm then hooks back upward as the body completes its turn and the left arm crashes vertically with the back of the hand facing down.

4.   Alternate. The body turns left as the punch folds downward while the hooking arm circles vertically to perform a punch.

The large detaining arm is an example of Cheung Bo's structure. It uses a powerful plucking motion to quickly suppress a heavy punch while the body moves around it to flank and the arm relaxes back up, assuming a hooking shape to maintain control. As the relatively open nature

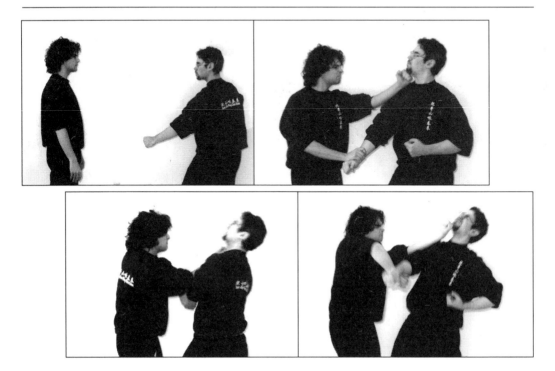

Antony stops Rene's attack with a grasping arm thrusting punch. Rene retaliates with a swing and Antony uses the detaining joining arm to suppress the attack. When Rene tries to recover, Antony again employs the joining detaining arm to counter.

of this detaining arm leaves the ribs exposed, the turning of the body also serves to place them out of harm's way. Depending on the strike being intercepted, the detaining arm can range from a subtle control, to a stinging slap, to a cutting pluck.

The large circle hanging punch here illustrates the "linked defense and attack" qualities of the technique as it can simultaneously strike, close the body in a vertical manner, and be used to help control and suppress an opponent's bridge.

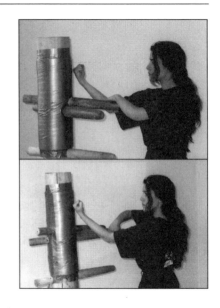

扣
攬
手

Detaining Grasping Arms
Kao lop sao (detaining grasping arms) employs the grasping arm to maintain control of the opponent's bridge.

Flapping Wing Palms

扑翼掌

Pok yik jeung (flapping wing palms) combines turning power with horizontal palms that can attack or defend simultaneously, as needed. It can be trained in a variety of manners, both inside and outside, and while stationary or moving. The moving version, which contains some elements not previously mentioned, is presented below.

Flapping Wing Palms

1. Open the form.

2. Step and raise the arm. The left leg steps forward and to the outside while the left hand performs a supporting palm and the other hand remains guarding.

3. Step and swing the palm. The right leg circles forward and back in as the body turns right and both arms swing horizontally, palms facing the same direction and fingers pointing forward.

4. Alternate. The right leg steps outward as the right hand executes a supporting palm to begin the sequence on the other side.

When Georgia charges forward, Rene uses the moving horse to angle in while covering her arm with the supporting palm. Rene then slams Georgia with the connected power of the flapping wing palms, uprooting her.

The outside step is part of the *yee ma* (moving horse), found formally in the biu jee and later forms. There are several different versions of the moving horse, used to travel in a variety of angular and circular ways. The initial, more linear setup step helps introduce important concepts of positioning. The circling step aspect aids in setting up the proper placement to check the opponent's lower body and disrupt his or her structure.

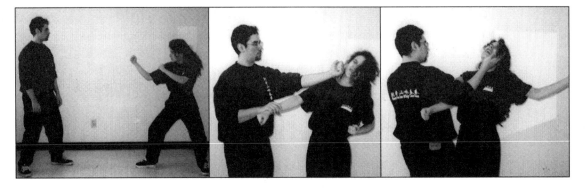

Rene counters Geogia's attack with a grasping arm hanging punch. As Georgia tries to attack again with a swing, one of Rene's flapping wing palms strikes her bridge, stopping the attack, while the other strikes her jaw.

After stopping Georgia's initial attack with a grasping arm thrusting punch. Rene steps in and applies the flapping wing palms.

The flapping wing palms, in various forms, are also found in the wooden dummy set. They can be applied defensively or offensively, with short, shocking power or with longer, uprooting power.

In a historical context, uprooting applications were developed for use aboard the boats and narrow alleys and rooms of southern China. Under such conditions, the long power of movements like the flapping wing palms could send an opponent reeling face first into a wall or careening off the side of a boat and into the water, rapidly ending an encounter. In a modern context, uprooting applications can be used to disrupt an opponent in order create openings for rapid follow-ups.

The flapping wing palms can be used to train both footwork and waist power on the wooden dummy.

Sticking Single Bridge

黏
單
橋

Na dan kiu (sticking single bridge) cycles a sinking bridge technique with a punch in a set designed to train the dissolving of heavy force. This exercise helps train practitioners to maintain their structure while under pressure and while turning.

1. Open the form.

2. Turn and lower the arm. The body turns roughly 45 degrees to the left as the left arm sinks downward to a position just below the navel.

3. Turn and punch. The body turns back to the front and the left arm punches as it rises and travels back to the center.

The downward movement of the arm represents a chum kiu (sinking bridge), as seen in the form of the same name. In this set, it uses the connected power of the horse, waist, and arm to dissolve a heavy force. In cases of higher attacks, a higher barring motion can be used.

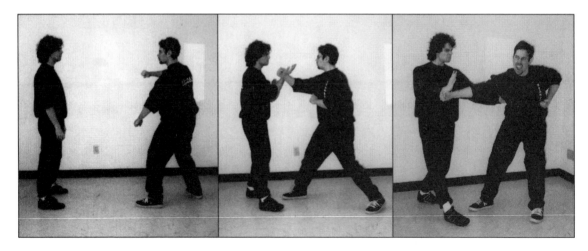

Antony begins to intercept Rene's punch with a dispersing arm. When Rene tries to power his way through, however, Antony redirects his force with the sticking single bridge and counters with a thrusting punch.

White Crane Seizes the Fox

白
鶴
擒
狐

Bak hok kum wu (white crane seizes the fox) uses chasing steps to maintain control of an opponent, and the arms and legs, like scissors to cut them down. This illustrates wing chun kuen's chasing body principles and the use of three bridges at once.

1. Open the form.

2. Step and intercept. The right leg moves with a toe-out step as the right arm per forms an outside join.

3. Kick and extend the bridge. The body turns to the right as the left leg kicks forward and the left arm moves out.

4. Step and alternate. When alternating, the kicking leg steps toe-out while the chopping arm changes to the outside join.

The initial step can be used to gain proper positioning while the outside join (or more commonly in application, the outside grasp) gains control of the opponent's upper body.

Antony lunges forward with a swing. Rene controls him with a grasping arm while at the same time cutting him down with a killing bridge and angle horse.

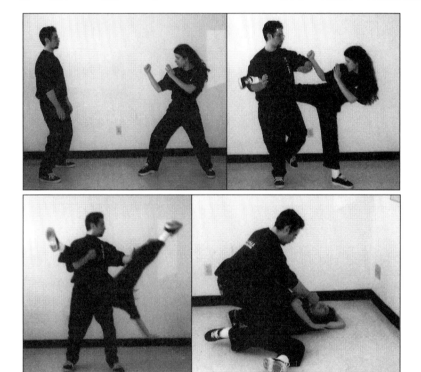

Rene controls Georgia's side kick and takes her down with white crane seizes the fox. He then follows up with a kneeling side punch.

The *gwok ma* (angle horse) is a short, powerful kick typically used to sweep an opponent's leg.

Saat kiu (killing bridge), often used in the application of this set, is also found in the biu jee form. Here, it chops horizontally in the opposite direction to the angle horse, effectively cutting down an opponent.

The chasing horse aspect of the technique can be used to follow and control an opponent who tries to gain range for an attack.

Variations of this form include controlling with a shovel bridge and pressing leg, etc.

White crane seizes the fox, drilled on the wooden dummy.

CHAPTER 7

Little First Training

Siu lien tao (little first training) is the first linked long form of Yuen Kay-San wing chun kuen. A stationary exercise practiced while in the trapezoid-shaped clamping groin horse throughout, it concentrates on developing stability and balance, linking body structure, basic bridge arms, and the *chuen ging* (inch power) of the bridges.

Siu lien (xiao lian) is an old name used in several Siu Lam (Shaolin) related styles. The first character refers to "little or small." The second encompasses "training, practice, or drilling." To this is added *tao,* meaning "beginning, first, or head." Thus, it can be theorized that the *siu lien tao* begins the practitioners training with the little elements—the conceptual points. This includes the physical work the body must go through to learn the relaxation, positions, structures, and powers. It also includes the mental development of intention and combining this with the physical work.

Grandmaster Sum Nung has stated that "Every time you practice the *siu lien tao,* your wing chun kuen gets one step better." This helps illustrate the fundamental importance of the form and its consistent practice.

Siu lien tao is typically taught in sections. This allows the practitioner to concentrate and develop each one before having to worry about the whole. Since names and labels sometimes vary from one wing chun kuen branch to another, for the purposes of this book, when no clear standard term could be found names of representative movements have been used.

In addition to a slightly longer opening form, the *siu lien tao* consists of the following eight sections: 1) cross-shaped arms; 2) three prayers to Buddha; 3) pinning arms; 4) darting fingers; 5) circling bridges; 6) swallowing arms; 7) wing arms; and 8) three-star punch.

The *siu lien tao* can also be practiced in the *duk gerk ma* (single leg horse) throughout. The single leg horse, as its name implies, has the entire body supported on one leg while the other leg is brought up until the thigh is parallel to the ground. Training the form in the single leg horse helps develop balance and the structure of the leg.

Opening Form

The opening of the *siu lien tao* contains a few elements in addition to the standard opening.

Opening form

1. Open the form.

2. Cross the arms. The hands open and chop downwards until the wrists cross on the meridian line.

3. Rotate the arms. The hands move inwards and upwards, closing into fists, before crashing back down to blend into the withdrawal motion.

4. Withdraw the arms.

The downward motion of the bridges represents a duel version of the cultivating arms seen in the triangle palms form. In application, one or the other is used separately but the double movement in the form helps the practitioner develop proper placement on the meridian line.

The rotation of the arms following the crossing arms demonstrates the large hanging punch, the secondary punching technique of the system.

Gaun sao gwa choi (cultivating arm hanging punch) is another early *san sao* drill that employs the cultivating arm and a simultaneous hanging punch (or thrusting punch) with the 45-degree side horse. An extension of the high and low cultivating arms section of the *biu jee* form, it is introduced early for its value in beginners training. Although the cultivating arm hanging punch covers the lower body, its principles and practice are similar to those of the barring arm thrusting punch.

Ngo sifu demontrates the cultivating arm hanging punch, another of the first san sao drills commonly taught in the system. Georgia then applies the movement to deal with successive low round-house attacks.

Cross Shaped Arm

十
字
手

The *siu lien tao* begins with the core punch and a series of movements that work the wrist through the basic angles for both flexibility and power, offense and defense. It also introduces the pushing palm and the fanning version of the grasping arm.

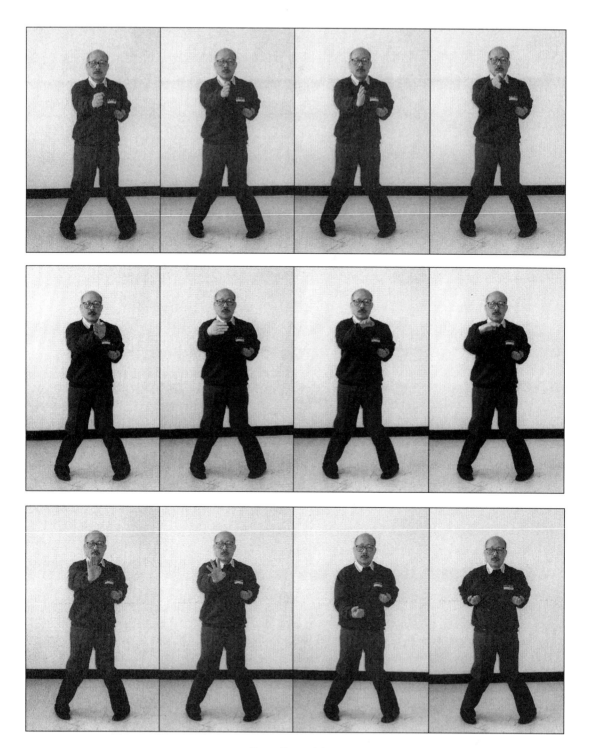

Cross Shaped Arm

1. Extend the punch. From the chambered position the left arm executes a meridian punch.

2. Rotate the wrist. The left fist opens, pointing the fingers straight outward. Keeping the elbow and fingers immobile, the wrist then sinks downward, rises upward, pushes inward, pushes outward, turns over and moves inward, and finally moves outward.

3. Extend the palm. The palm pushes forward until the arm is extended and the fingers point up.

4. Turn the hand and close the fist. The hand turns outward while the fingers fan out before closing into a fist.

5. Withdraw and punch. The right arm begins to strike as the left arm drops downward to start its withdrawal.

6. Alternate. Repeat the sequence with the right arm.

The series of movements following the meridian punch are known as *sup jee sao* (cross-shaped arm) which describes the basic motion of the wrist. *Sup jee* represents the "shape of the Chinese character *sup*" which is composed of a vertical line crossing a horizontal line (identical to the + sign in mathematics). This represents the basic wrist motions used for defense and offense. Training both the flexibility and inch power of the wrist, each movement can serve as a redirection or a strike.

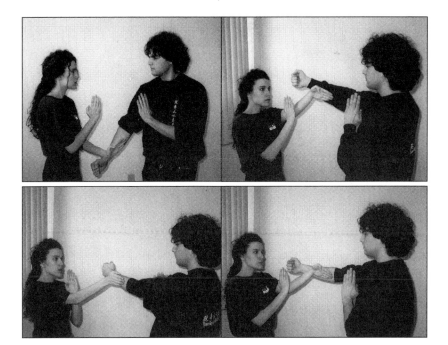

Georgia demonstrates some of the basic defensive angles trained by the cross shaped arm, including down, up, inside, and outside.

It is said that in the *siu lien tao* form of Fok Bo-Chuen, the movements following the opening meridian punch consisted of three inward circles performed with the palm facing down. Known as *sae ying sao* (snake-shape arm), Yuen Kay-San felt that separating and clarifying the techniques would improve the sequence. This refinement eventually led to the cross-shaped arm. Today, some of the *siu lien tao* forms descending from early students of grandmaster Sum Nung, such as Kwok Jin-Fen, retain elements of the snake form arm in their sequence.

The *toi jeung* (pushing palm) that follows the cross shaped arm trains the pressing method for applying power through the center of the hand.

The grasping arm that precedes the withdrawal helps train the flexibility needed to seize bridges well positioned on the meridian line but is similar in function to the version seen in the *sup yee sik* of the same name. In addition to its usefulness in *kum na* (*qin na,* seizing and holding), it can function as *fan kum na* (counter seizing and holding) using leverage to reverse arm grappling attempts.

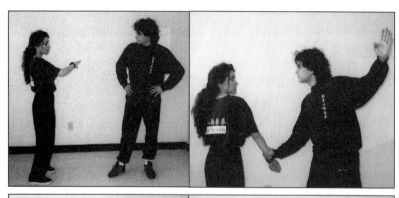

Antony grabs Georgia's arm and raises his hand to strike her. Georgia uses the grasping arm to reverse his hold while she moves in, locking his arm and breaking his structure.

Three Prayers to Buddha

三
拜
佛

The second section opens with several points that train the vital alignment of the bridges on the meridian line. The section also contains motions for covering both the inside and outside, and continues the development of wrist flexibility and power.

Three prayers to Buddha

1. Align the palm. The left fist opens and the hand comes forward along the body, palm facing up, thumb side facing forward. It comes to rest with the center of the palm on the meridian line a short distance in front of the body (enough to prevent the elbow from flaring).

2. Snap the palm. While the elbow remains unmoving, the palm snaps upward.

3. Extend the arm. The elbow moves onto the meridian line, extending the bridge to form a dispersing arm.

4. Rotate the wrist. The wrist rotates, bringing the fingers inward.

5. Sink the wrist. Keeping the fingertips in place, the wrist sinks downward until the fingers are pointing up.

6. Retract the bridge. The elbow withdraws slightly, staying in. The fingers stay pointing up and the hand remains on the meridian line until it assumes a position just in front of the body.

7. Snap the wrist. The wrist snaps forward and the fingers fold in toward the body.

8. Extend the arm. The elbow again extends along the meridian line with the wrist remaining bent into position and the fingers staying centered.

9. Sink the wrist. The finger tips remain in place while the wrist sinks downward until the fingers are pointing up.

10. Retract the bridge. The elbow withdraws slightly, staying in. The fingers stay pointing up and the hand remains on the meridian line until it assumes a position just in front of the body.

11. Repeat. Steps 7 through 10 are repeated twice more.

12. Push the palm. Following the last retraction of the bridge, the hand pushes to the side just in front of the shoulder to form a supporting palm.

13. Circle the bridge. Keeping the fingers pointing forward, the bridge arcs horizontally, bringing the hand to shoulder width and nose height.

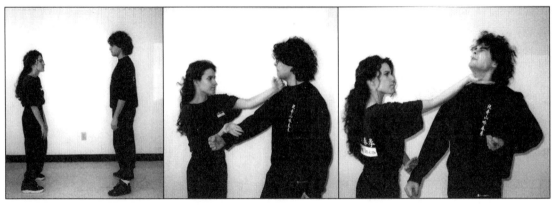

Georgia intercepts Antony 's punch with a dispersing hit and follows up with a butting palm to his throat.

When Antony grabs Georgia's arm, she reverses with a circling arm and counters with a throat locking technique.

14. Chop the palm edge downward. The circling continues and the hand returns to the meridian line before crashing down to assume a relatively straight position at shoulder height.

15. Shift the wrist. The wrist moves inward and then outward.

16. Push the palm, grasp, and withdraw.

17. Alternate. Perform the sequence with the right arm.

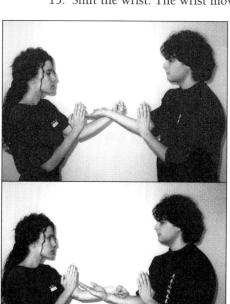

The initial upward snapping of the palm works to train the inch power of the *ding jeung* (butting palm). The rotation of the wrist that follows can represent a middle-level version of the circling arm and is well suited for counter seizing and holding. The sinking motion can be used to redirect incoming force downward when already in contact.

The partial withdrawal of the arm trains the *wu sao* (guarding arm). The guarding arm is the second line of defense and moves to quickly intercept any attacks that manage to get past the primary joining bridge (becoming a supporting palm should anything get past the dispersing arm, a dispersing arm should anything get by the supporting palm, and so forth).

The forward snapping of the wrist helps to train the inch power of the *da sao ging* (hitting wrist).

The next extension of the bridge demonstrates another version of the controlling arm. This one can be used to maintain control after having been intercepted by a motion such as the dispersing arm.

In this drill, as Antony tries to parry Georgia's punch with a dispersing arm she remains flexible and assumes the controlling arm. When Antony tries to punch through, Georgia uses the sinking bridge to dissipate it.

Georgia cuts into Antony's swinging attack with a barring arm and strikes with a palm to his brachial plexus. She then follows up with a wrist strike to his chin.

The above controlling and guarding movements are commonly referred to as *sam pai fut* (three prayers to Buddha), since the guarding arm resembles a position of worship. Perhaps coincidentally, this reportedly was also the name of Fung Siu-Ching's original weng chun boxing form that blended characteristics of the tree wing chun boxing forms. During training, the three prayers to Buddha section should be executed "so slowly that no movement is perceptible, yet there is still movement."

The arcing motion that follows is the first of two such actions in the form. This one, the smaller of the circling bridges, can be used to subtlety join with and redirect incoming force.

Po jeung (cleaving palm) crashes down the meridian line, expressing penetrating inch power with the side of the hand.

Pinning Arms

The third section trains the downward power of the bridges in all directions around the body. It also works the contraction and expansion of the torso and the opening and closing motions to the side.

1. Press the arms down to the sides. From the chambered position, both fists open and the palms turn downward. The arms then press downward at the sides with the fingers facing naturally out.

Pinning Arms

2. Press the arms down to the back. After retracting partially, the arms press down behind the body with the fingers facing forward.

3. Press the arms down to the front. After retracting partially again, the arms press down in front of the body.

4. Swing the arms out. From the forward position, the arms swing up and outward in a vertical arc before the elbows drop down at the sides, bringing the hands to shoulder level.

5. Fold the arms in. Moving horizontally, the arms fold inward until the backs of the hands touch the body and the elbows point forward.

6. Withdraw. Similar to the re-chambering performed at the end of the opening sequence, both arms crash downward in the large version of the hanging punch before withdrawing.

In the olden days, it was said that the power of the palms in this section, if practiced on the second floor, should cause the whole house to shake. With the stability of modern constructions, this goal may be almost impossible to achieve but the symbolism remains helpful.

The pressing movements can be used as *on sao* (pinning arms). The word *on* means to "press, push downward, or pin down" and reflects an aspect of the power trained by these motions.

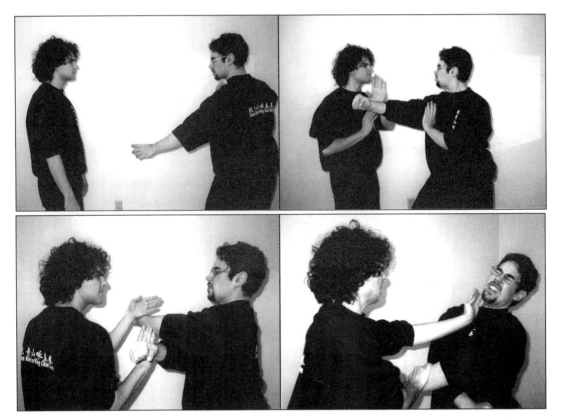

Antony displaces Rene's first punch at the last moment with a supporting palm. When Rene punches again, Antony maintains contact with one arm while the other circles to swallow the force. With Rene's bridges crossed, Antony controls them both with one hand and counters with a chopping palm.

The sideways press is commonly used as counter seizing and holding to dissolve arm-locking attempts. By rapidly extending the arm, and following with a rotation such as the saving arm, the opponent's locking force can be disrupted and the practitioner's limb freed.

The backward palms can likewise be used in this manner, and as such was also taught with the fingers pointing out away from the body to better emphasize the counter seizing and holding aspect of the movement. It can also be used to strike out at a target behind the body.

The forward press can be used following a detaining arm to keep a bridge suppressed. It can also be used to push downward an opponent who comes in low.

The initial motion of the vertical arc represents a large version of the outside join sometimes used to change the bridge from an inside position to an outside position (such as an inside wing arm to outside grasping arm). It can also be used as a way to uproot and take down an opponent.

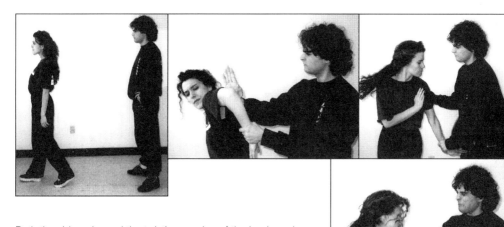

Both the side palm and the twisting version of the backward palm can be used for counter-seizing and and holding. In this application, Antony grabs Geogia's arm from the back and moves to lock it. Georgia reacts by spiraling her arm downnward, releasing the grab. She then turns and follows up with a thrust punch

Antony approaches Georgia from behind and goes to grab her. Georgia immediately slams her palms backward, disrupting her attacker. Seizing the opportunity, Georgia quickly turns and strikes with a hacking elbow.

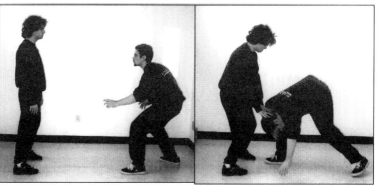

When Rene shoots in on Antony, Antony makes contact and sinks his posture and arms onward, directing Rene into the ground.

The end part of the movement can function as *lok jaan* (dropping elbow), parrying an attack directed below the bridge while simultaneously striking its more sensitive areas. In addition, it can be used to strike at a downward target.

The horizontal movement of the elbows can function as a form of running arm used to evade a grabbing attempt. In addition, it can represent a close body version of the *pai jaan* (hacking elbow) seen in the *chum kiu* and wooden dummy forms. Linearly, the motion can also be employed as a *ding jaan* (butting elbow).

Rene, distracted, reacts instinctively with a wing arm when he sees Antony's arm flying towards him from the corner of his eye. Realizing a follow up is imminent, Rene uses an outside join to change position and counters with a hanging punch.

Rene jabs toward Antony who moves in right away and breaks Rene's structure with a wing arm. Antony then controls RenÈ's bridge while simultaneously using the large outside join to throw him to the ground.

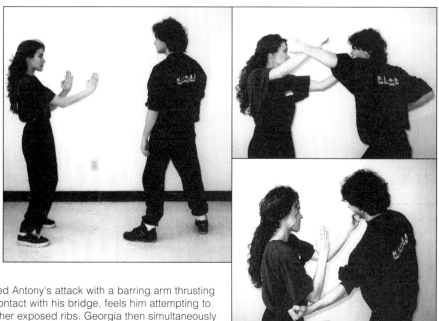

Georgia, having countered Antony's attack with a barring arm thrusting punch and maintained contact with his bridge, feels him attempting to swing around and strike her exposed ribs. Georgia then simultaneously stops and strikes the attack with a dropping elbow while countering.

As Antony shuffles forward with a side kick, Georgia turns her center out of the path of attack and strikes Antony's ankle with a dropping elbow. As Antony's foot comes down, she slices in and strikes before leveraging him to the ground.

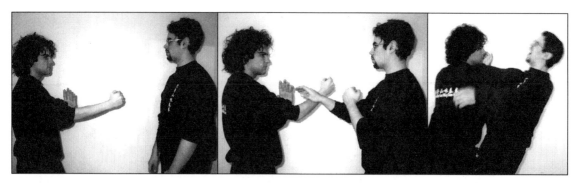

When Rene tries to grab Antony's bridge and pull him, Antony goes with the pull, staying locked on Rene's center, and strikes him with a butting elbow.

Darting Fingers

鏢
指

Section four works a variety of movements that project power forward, downward, and upward. It also introduces techniques that illustrate the leaking and darting methods of the system.

1. Extend the arms. The fists open slightly, leaving the fingers pointing naturally upward, and the arms extend forward.

2. Rotate the wrists and thrust the hands forward. As the elbows come onto the meridian line, the wrists rotate, turning the palms downward while darting them forward at eye level.

3. Press the arms downward. Similar to the forward pressing motion of the previous section, this version begins higher and arcs slightly inward at midpoint before finishing its descent.

4. Raise the wrists upward. The wrists rise upward, keeping a natural bend in the elbows, until the hands are roughly at chin level.

5. Withdraw. Resembling the first re-chambering performed in the opening sequence, both arms perform the small circle hanging punch before withdrawing.

The initial extension of the arm can serve to bridge at a level lower then that of the dispersing arm.

The rotation of the wrists can be used as a form of *lao sao* (leaking arm) to counter changes like a circling arm. It can also be employed to scoop up attacks such as high kicks.

The outward motion of the fingers is an example of a palm down *biu jee* (darting fingers) that can be targeted at an opponent's vulnerable areas. Like the meridian punch, it can also disperse or control as it strikes.

A form of detaining arm precedes the pinning arm in this section. The slight arcing action serves to subtly decelerate an opponent's attack and swallow the force during the redirection.

The upward wrist movement can illustrate a vertical version of the hitting wrist performed in the second section.

Darting fingers section

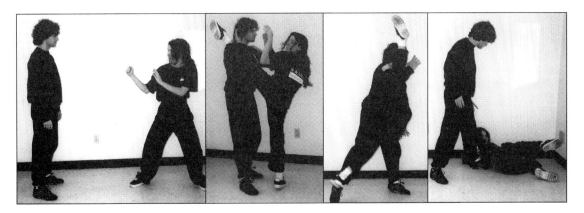

When Georgia kicks at Antony's head, Antony scoops up her leg and drops her on the ground.

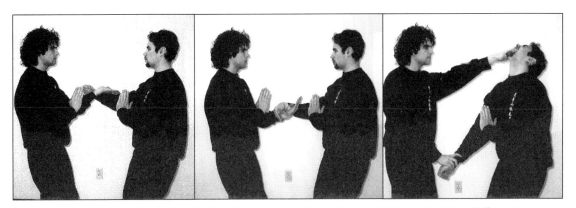

Antony parries Rene's punch with a dispersing arm. Rene tries to clear the parry with a circling arm, but Antony leaks around and strikes with darting fingers.

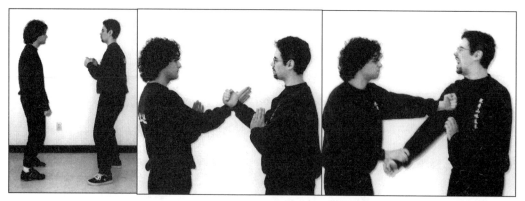

Rene makes contact with Antony's bridge and tries to force his way through. Antony swallows Rene's power with an arcing detaining arm and counters with a thrusting punch.

Circling Bridges

A larger version of the movements found following the three prayers to Buddha is contained in the fifth section. It also contains motions that train the pushing, pressing, and striking power of the palms.

1. Push the Palm. This version of the supporting palm is executed at solar plexus level and further in front of the body.

2. Circle the bridge. The arm arcs horizontally in a larger version of the circling bridge, remaining at shoulder height throughout.

3. Extend the palm. As the arm circles back to the meridian line, the palm pushes forward at shoulder height.

4. Extend the fingers. Following the palm, the fingers push forward at throat level.

5. Extend the palm. After the finger press, a second palm extension strikes forward.

6. Grasp and withdraw. A grasping arm is executed before the arm re-chambers.

7. Alternate. Now perform the sequence with the right arm.

The horizontal circling bridge in this section, slightly wider and lower than its predecessor, is ideal for use with larger footwork patterns.

The first pushing palm and the darting fingers extension illustrate furtherance of the progressive, pressing approach to uprooting an opponent. The second palm motion works on developing the inch power of the strike.

Chan jee pai (paper pressing) is a drill used to develop the pushing palm and similar power. It uses the concept of pressing in both vertical and horizontal exercises.

Circling Bridges

As Rene punches, Antony steps inside and employs a supporting palm.
Rene, seeing Antony exposed, attacks again but Antony remains in
contact and continues to advance, using a circling bridge to stop the
second punch. With Rene drawn completely open, Antony retaliates
with a pressing palm and thrusting fingers.

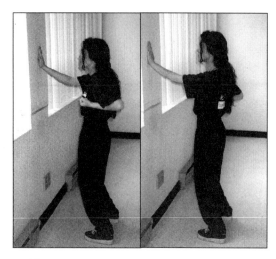

Georgia practices pressing power.

Swallowing Arms

The sixth section trains spiraling power up and down the meridian line. It also introduces lower versions of the palm and grasping arm.

1. Extend the bridge and twist the hand. The left hand opens and extends along the meridian line to nose level. As it extends, the bridge twists to the outside.

2. Drop the bridge. Keeping the hand on the meridian line, the bridge cuts downward assuming a position below the navel.

3. Raise the bridge and twist the hand. The bridge rises again to assume the same position as the first motion.

4. Lower the arm and rotate the wrist. The arm again falls downward along the meridian line, this time moving outward until the elbow is at the hip, the wrist slightly below, and the fingers point downward.

5. Rotate the wrist and extend the arm. Without pause, the wrist continues to rotate while the bridge extends along the meridian line, striking forward with the edge of the palm.

6. Grasp and withdraw. The hand then rotates, bringing the fingers slightly up. A grasping arm is executed before the arm is withdrawn.

7. Alternate. Perform the sequence with the right arm.

Known as *tun sao* (swallowing arm), this first technique can be employed in a similar manner to the dispersing arm, although its twisting nature helps build a different kind of inch power and gives it an advantage in certain force dispersal and counter seizing and holding situations.

Swallowing arms

Rene steps forward and grabs Georgia's arm. Georgia twists her bridge into the swallowing arm. This breaks Rene's structure, allowing Georgia to shoot under with a throat locking arm.

Fai jee gung (chopstick work) can help train the twisting power of the bridges. The implement itself is composed of a bundle of rounded chopsticks. Training is accomplished by twisting the bundle up and down from a double swallowing arm to double detaining arm position.

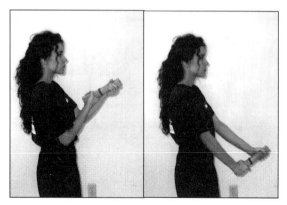

Georgia trains twisting power with the chopstick bundle.

Utilizing sinking power, the *po jung sao* (center-cleaving arm) can be employed to quickly cut down the meridian line and intercept attacks coming in below the bridges when not initially in contact with the opponent.

The initial movement following the second swallowing arm can be used as a detaining arm to pluck downward mid-level attacks, while the latter part can serve as a circling arm to change the bridge from inside to out or outside to in, or to spread lower forces to the side.

Also derived from this movement, the *seung huen sao* (double circling arms) is a basic sticking platform used to develop sensitivity. One partner begins in a double dispersing arm position. The other begins in double controlling arms and uses the circling arm to split open the other person's bridges. Both partners should endeavor to keep the elbows in against the ribs. Beginning changes from the dispersing arm include a pinning arm in response to a low palm strike and a wing arm in response to a thrusting punch. Changes from the circling arm include the high controlling arm in response to a thrusting punch.

While Antony is talking, Rene attacks with a low punch. Seeing the movement, Antony strikes it with a center cleaving arm and counters with a thrusting punch.

The *dai jeung* (low palm) is used to strike an opponent's waist area while the low level grasping arm can be employed to attack the groin in a version of "monkey plucking peaches."

Georgia intercepts Rene's punch with an inside join. Moving to the outside with a circling bridge, she covers with a supporting palm and counters with a low palm strike.

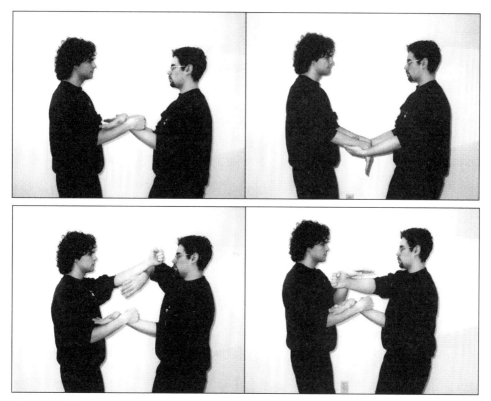

Antony and Rene practice double circling arms, an early sticking arms platform. From the double controlling arm position, Antony splits Rene's double dispersing arms with circling arms. The circling continues smoothly until the arms resume the starting position. Simple changes in the exercise include warding off a punch with a wing arm or inside join.

Wing Arm

Section seven presents another version of the wing arm, develops the closing of the sinking elbow saving arm, and completes the variations of palm and grasping arm sequences.

1. Spiral the arm forward. The left fist opens and the arm spirals forward to assume the high-level wing arm.

2. Drop the arm. The elbow drops downward to a position beside the ribs with the wrist just below and slightly inward.

3. Raise the palm. The arm shoots forward and upward along the meridian line. The palm ends roughly in line with the chin.

4. Grasp and withdraw. The hand then rotates, bringing the fingers slightly up. A grasping arm is executed before the arm is withdrawn.

5. Alternate. Perform the sequence with the right arm.

Wing arm section

While similar in final position to the wing arm in the single dragon and arrow punch forms, the execution of the movement differs. Rather than sweeping upward to clear the torso, it is thrown forward to intercept and disrupt an incoming bridge.

The wing arm is often used in sticking training as well. *Gwai bong* (rolling wings) trains a cycle of the wing arm, grasping arm, detaining arm, and hanging punch. A simple sticking drill, it helps reinforce the concepts of "a wing arm never stops or stays" and "when you meet a wing arm you must detain it." It also trains raising the elbow when the wrist is pulled down, maintaining contact during changes, simultaneous attack and suppression, and other important elements.

The dropping arm represents the *chum jaan gao sao* (sinking elbow saving arm) which trains the body to reflexively close openings before an opponent can take advantage of them. Examples include closing the ribs to prevent a punch from striking below the bridge or dissolving the force of an attempted joint-lock.

The palm executed following the saving arm is usually applied at a lower level than it is practiced in form.

Georgia controls Rene's attack with a grasping arm hanging punch. When Rene tries to counter with a swing, Georgia intercepts, moves to the outside, and strikes with a low palm. A deadlier counter could include a version of "monkey picking peach."

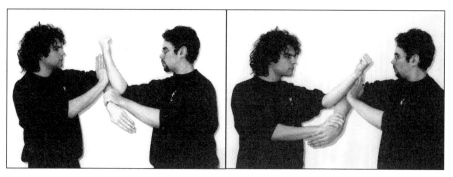

Another early sticking arms platform moves from the protecting arm and wing arm to the detaining arm and hanging punch.

Three Star Punch

The final section of the *siu lien tao* trains slicing power both downward and outward and finishes where it began, further elaborating the concepts of the punch.

1. Cross the bridges downward. The hands open while the elbows come out and both arms travel downward until the wrists cross on the meridian line, right bridge on top of left.

2. Alternate bridges. The left elbow retracts upward, taking position roughly in front of the shoulder. The left arm then descends back down while the right arm rises upward. The left elbow then rises again while the right arm descends.

3. Chain punch. Beginning with the right arm, three chain punches are executed, one with rising power, one sinking, and one level. On the last punch, the left arm retracts completely.

4. Withdraw. The right arm performs a grasping arm and re-chambers.

While the initial motion resembles the low crossed cultivating arms in the opening sequence, the execution differs in that the arms do not swing from the elbow. Rather, they make use of slicing power along a linear, vertical path. The movement can serve to train the *chan kiu* (shoveling bridges) found in the wooden dummy set.

The chain punches, known as *sam sing choi* (three star punch), help illustrate methods of simultaneous interception and attack with the punch.

Three star punch

As Rene steps forward to attack, Antony immediately moves in, controls his arm,
and slices into his center with a shoveling over bridge.

CHAPTER 8

The Closing Form

收
式

The sao sik (closing form) is performed at the end of all the routines in Yuen Kay-San wing chun kuen. As its name implies, the closing form is the complement of the opening form. While the opening form introduces the basics of boxing to practitioners and readies them for training, the closing form returns them to a relaxed and centered position following their practice. This applies to both the mind and body.

Closing Form

1. Rotate the heels in. The feet rotate on the front until the heels come together.

2. Rotate the toes in. The feet then rotate on heels until the toes also come together.

3. Raise the posture. The knees straighten, raising the body to a natural standing position.

4. Turn the palms down. The hands open and the palms turn to face down.

5. Press the palms down. The palms drop downward until the arms are naturally extended.

6. Ending position. The arms relax with the fingers pointing down.

The closing of the trapezoid-shaped clamping groin horse returns a practitioner to a natural standing position. Any urge to hurry through the end should be resisted and this section should be trained at the same pace and with the same intention as the rest of the form.

The lowering of the palms, while resembling the side pinning arms near the beginning of the form, are not done with the explosive power of those movements but in a relaxed manner. When a form is completed, practitioners can choose to repeat it and further refine its movements or explore another form and train other elements.

PART FOUR

練
功

Training

CHAPTER 9

Basic Training

The term kung-fu reflects "skill achieved by hard work over a period of time." In short, it deals with training. Only through training can the system of wing chun kuen be realized by a practitioner.

As stated previously, wing chun kuen is not a broad art with dozens of long sequences to learn and set combinations to memorize. It is a deep art that presents its core concepts in a few profound routines. Thus, each point is important and must serve many different purposes. They function in attribute development (building relaxation, flexibility, body alignment, refined muscle use, etc.), defense (reducing an opponent's possible angles from the outset, intercepting bridges in motion, restricting extended bridges, etc.), and offense (striking, locking, throwing, etc. with all parts of the body).

To fully explore the depth and potential of each point requires intelligence, creativity, and perseverance on the part of the practitioner. This exploration works on refining each point (both singularly and in combination) by oneself in solo practice or with another person in partner training.

No matter the type of training, a practitioner should be sure to begin slowly and gradually increase in a step-by-step manner as skill develops.

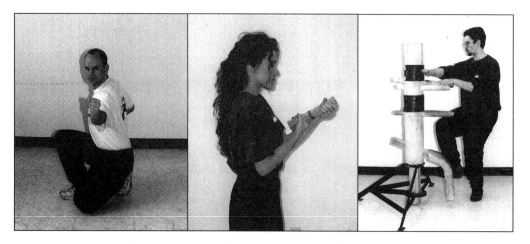

Wing chun kuen solo training includes practice of the points by themselves and linked together, as well as with equipment such as the chopstick bundle and wooden dummy.

Solo Training

Solo training ranges from the simple drilling of individual moves, to combinations of motions, to choreographed forms and the use of training equipment. Since wing chun kuen does not require much space in which to practice, solo training can be done often and under many different circumstances.

Drills

Drills are the building blocks of training. Each core conceptual motion contained in wing chun kuen can be isolated and polished, drilled until it becomes reflexive. From there, points can be combined together in almost limitless variety and trained until they flow from one to the other according to conditions.

Forms

The forms of wing chun kuen link together the individual motions and concepts to help the practitioner remember the material and provide a progressive manner in which to develop it. Thus, the short sets of the sup yee sik and the long routines such as siu lien tao serve as catalogs and guidelines for all the essential points of the system.

Training Work

Lien gung sik (training work forms) are used to help build the attributes of wing chun kuen. Training work also allows the practitioner to drill movements and power levels not practical or unsafe for a living partner. In wing chun kuen, training equipment includes mirrors, sandbags, candles, rattan rings, chopstick bundles, paper, and the famed wooden dummy.

Partner Training

 No matter how much one may practice on his or her own or with training equipment, wing chun kuen is an application oriented art and can only be fully realized through drilling with a real, responsive, partner. In wing chun kuen, *san sao* (separate techniques) and *chi sao* (sticking arms) provide a structured, progressive method for such training.

Extreme care should be given to not allowing partner training to become a competition. If "winning" becomes the goal, the real purpose and benefit of the exercise is lost. The true goal of partner training is the development of bridging and sensitivity, and the internalization of changes. This can only be accomplished in a progressive, cooperative manner. When mistakes are made they should be analyzed, understood, and drilled until they are overcome. An effort should also be made to practice with as many different partners with as many varying body types as possible. Friendly practice with partners from other branches and even systems is also an important part of development.

Separate Techniques
San sao (separate techniques) involve the practice of wing chun kuen motions, both individually and in combination, where no pre-existing contact exists. The nature of san sao ranges from the repetitive practice of basic motions to simple bridging and countering maneuvers to a freestyle exchange of techniques.

While sooner or later all motions in wing chun kuen must be taken apart and explored through san sao, in the beginning there are several semi-formal sets that are introduced. Barring arm thrusting punch, cultivating arm hanging punch, and other early san sao drills help give novice practitioners some basic tools they can use while working on developing the sensitivity required for more refined wing chun kuen application.

Sticking Arms
Chi sao (sticking arms) is one of the most famed aspects of wing chun kuen. Like san sao, sticking arms is a dynamic and ever-changing laboratory through which wing chun kuen techniques are deconstructed and explored in application. Chi sao, however, focuses this exploration on the development of the reflexes used when the bridges are already in contact. At this extremely close range, eyesight can sometimes be too slow to adapt to a fast opponent and feeling and reflex become paramount.

Two person san sao training ranges from the practice of single points, both alone and with a partner, to application drills.

There is a saying in wing chun kuen that "sticking arms is like asking the way." In this sense, every wing chun kuen bridge is really a question posed to the opponent. If they do not respond, they can be struck. If they do, the bridge will change (based on feeling) and ask again. Thus, it is actually the opponent who sets up his or her own defeat.

As with san sao, sticking arms begins with simple drills and exercises, such as the double circling arms, rolling wings, and the famed luk sao (rolling arms). At first, partners work to develop and maintain their body structure and sense defects in others. Later, changes are introduced and the openings they find exploited. This continues until the drill becomes a free-flowing exchange of techniques, with the bridges simply joining and going from there.

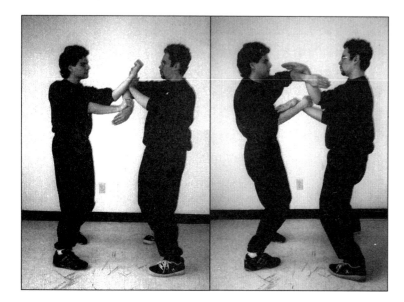

Chi sao practice includes the rolling wing drill and perhaps the most famous of wing chun kuen's exercises, the double rolling arms.

CHAPTER 10

Advanced Training

進級訓練

Although perhaps the most profound and important part of training, the material covered in the last few chapters have only scratched the surface of wing chun kuen. An intelligent system, the art can take practitioners as far as their tenacity and creativity leads them. To help guide a student on this path, the art includes numerous, more advanced, aspects.

Sinking Bridges

沉橋

Chum kiu (sinking bridges), the second fist form, follows the siu lien tao form in the curriculum. Similar to side punch and arrow punch that follow the meridian punch of the sup yee sik, this set integrates the basic motions with turning and stepping. Although both sinking (rooting) and bridging (joining) are trained in the form, the name itself is also said to hearken back to an old Siu Lam concept meaning to "sink the (opponent's) bridges," or in other words, to destroy their structure. The chum kiu form introduces kicking techniques such as heart piercing kick and side nailing kick. It also contains several different versions of the wing arm, sweeping and throwing performed at high, middle, and low levels, and versions of the barring arm, neck detaining arm, and other points.

Darting Fingers

鏢指

Biu jee (darting fingers), the third and final fist form, develops more advanced tactics. Biu jee can be interpreted as "darting with fingers" in that it works to develop a penetrating, exacting force. It can also be interpreted as "pointing," like a compass, in that it shows how to regain the center (control) when in tricky situations. Footwork in the biu jee form includes the moving horse while major sections consist of covering elbows, killing bridges, crossing arms, and saving body, among others.

Wooden Dummy

木人樁

The *mook yan jong* (wooden dummy) form contains movements from the three boxing forms and introduces motions such as butterfly palms, half-dispersing-half-wing, tiger tail kick, invisible kick, and the rising knee. Grandmaster Sum Nung also added in elements from the sup yee sik and refined it into a well-balanced set. The form itself is also practiced as *hong jong* (air dummy). This is simply the dummy form practiced on its own, without the actual physical dummy construct.

Kidney Breathing

腎氣歸元

Sun hei gwai yuen (kidney breathing invigoration, sometimes referred to as kidney breathing returns to source) are short hei gung (qigong, breathing/intrinsic energy work) like sets typically practiced after training to reenergize and revitalize the body. The kidney breathing sets include exercises like yielding breath, side-to-side waist, single hoof, expanding chest, dropping power, among others.

Low wing arm from the chum kiu form.

Cultivating arms from the biu jee form.

Butterfly palms from the muk yan jong & hong jong forms.

Expanding chest from the sun hei gwai yuen.

Six-and-a-Half-Point Pole

六
點
半
棍

Luk dim boon gwun (six-and-a-half-point pole) teaches the concepts of a long-handled, single-ended weapon. The single-headed pole used in wing chun kuen averages around eight feet in length and tapers toward the striking end. It is held with the hands a shoulder's width apart and is never spun nor twirled. It employs motions that require the practitioner to send power from their structure through the wood, out the striking point, and into the target. Rather than the standard wing chun kuen postures, pole training incorporates Siu Lam horses like the square horse and T-shaped horse. Pole techniques include six-and-a-half simple points and a few extensions like dispelling, spearing, whipping, two-motion, water-dripping, circling and pointing, barring, side-to-side, sitting-tail, fanning, among others, that cover all basic angles for both offense and defense. These are trained separately, combined, in form, using training devices such as balls suspended on string, small objects scattered on the floor, and later with partners in drills both structured and free-style.

Spearing pole from the luk dim boon gwun techniques.

Double Knives

一
字
雙
刀

Yee jee seung do (parallel-shaped double knives) train the use of twin short weapons. Their name is derived from their alternating in a yin and yang manner, never crossing near a practitioner's own arm (a dangerous practice in application). In wing chun kuen, the hands work like knives and the knives like hands. This means that skill with the blades follows skill achieved in the boxing. When applied the knives intercept or bar and cut the first available target, then move quickly to finish off an opponent. This finality of usage has also led them to be called by the more brutal name of *dit ming do* (life-taking knives).

Wing chun kuen knives are distinguished by their simplicity. They are never twirled nor spun about and are always held with the blades extended toward the opponent rather then folded back across the forearm as seen in other martial arts. With the fundamental drill of cultivating knives, a practitioner learns to wield, control, and change the two knives economically and efficiently while stationary and while moving in all directions. Subsequent motions introduce slicing, stabbing, barring, dispersing, cross shapes, wing, protecting, stealing and leaking, and other simple, elegant, yet frighteningly effective techniques.

A movement from the double knives

Afterword

By Georgia Dow

后
語

Whathat you have just read attempts to record the foundation of grandmaster Sum Nung's Yuen Kay-San wing chun kuen system as we learned it under our sifu, Ngo Lui-Kay. Even with the many early wake-up calls for photograph sessions, I am very happy to have been part of this process. I hope that you, the reader, have received half as much pleasure from reading this book as I have from my wing chun kuen training.

Training under Ngo sifu was always done with a minimum of intervention on his part. He would show us what to do and then watch us try to do it. He preferred us to feel our own mistakes and fix them ourselves. His presence, however, was always felt—a gentle nod or smile would tell us if we were on the right track. And when we truly met an impasse, he was always there to answer our questions.

Then, when we began to apply the concepts behind wing chun kuen to our training, we looked less and less to our teacher and focused more upon those concepts and their efficiency. Soon came the fateful day that we knew we would reach—to go out and learn to apply our wing chun kuen ourselves.

When our teacher told us that we were ready to go off on our own, I had a great feeling of loss. I didn't feel that I was ready to leave the nest and face the rest of my training without his direct guidance. There is a certain sense of security with a watchful eye looking over your shoulder, ensuring you don't stray too far from the correct path. Our teacher had always told us, however, not to take what he said as an absolute truth but to go and find out for ourselves. He told us that wing chun kuen is a thinking man's—a thinking person's—art and that we must learn for ourselves what is effective, in which situations, and why. This is what we did and continue to try to do. It is an ongoing process with every day bringing new learning opportunities. I am far from done in my wing chun kuen training and hope that I constantly learn more about its intricacies.

With the completion of this book, I must thank my parents, sifu, friends, classmates, and students. You have all made this a wonderful experience and may you all be as fortunate in your training.

Afterword

By Antony Casella

后
語

This book has indexed the way we learned the basic level of the art of Yuen Kay-San and grandmaster Sum Nung from our teacher, Ngo Lui-Kay. Like the wing chun kuen system, this book is to the art what a dictionary is to words.

When we first began studying wing chun kuen under Ngo sifu, each of us had experience in other martial arts. None of us, however, had ever been taught martial arts that were conceptually based (as opposed to technique oriented). In conceptually based martial arts, it is not about remembering 100 set patterns, but understanding a few ideas that can be manipulated into almost limitless applications. This proved to be a great hurdle at first. When we asked "Which way should this move be done?" Ngo sifu would respond "It depends on conditions." When this finally sank in, my personal ability in wing chun kuen and my ability to understand application improved. This was true not only for my own system but for others as well—I found I could "see" their concepts.

Gaining an understanding of wing chun kuen's concepts was not easy at first. Ngo sifu spoke only limited English and our knowledge of Chinese was non-existent. Two things helped greatly with this—Ngo sifu's patience and our classmate Rene's interest in Chinese language and history. When words were not enough, Ngo sifu used actions (usually accompanied by a smile or, more often than I would have liked, a frown.) When actions needed reinforcement, Ngo sifu would write things out and Rene would tackle them, dictionary in hand. It took time, especially at first, but eventually we all benefited from the research. I still don't know how he did it. How many of us could just pick up a dictionary and begin learning another language?

I don't believe that I would have the grasp of wing chun kuen I do now were it not for Rene's tenacity and love for the art. The reason for this, in part, is that wing chun kuen is a Chinese martial art and as such is the product of Chinese culture. To learn about that culture is to better understand the art.

With that in mind, it has been my pleasure to help in the production of this book. Although time consuming, it was well worth the effort. I would like to remind the reader, however, that no book could ever give that which is most important in wing chun kuen—the guidance of a good sifu. It is easy to look at a book and copy the movements, then say—"Ah ha! I know it!" However, this only scratches the surface. For this reason, anyone interested in the Yuen Kay-San system is urged to find qualified instruction. Although the art has been firmly established on most continents, it remains somewhat closed. For more information, please consult the Yuen Kay-San Wing Chun Kuen Homepage at http://www.wingchunkuen.com/yuenkaysan. In addition to historical and technical information, it contains periodically updated contact information for Yuen Kay-San wing chun kuen teachers around the world.

Ngo sifu was careful to tell us from the beginning that there was never a "one and only" way to do things, and to always look to the concepts when we weren't sure. "Maybe I'm right, maybe I'm wrong. I've taught you the concepts, now you have to think for yourselves," were his words. This advice was also empowering—it took away the ego and prejudice that all too often plagued our previous experiences in the martial arts. This meant Ngo sifu had given us the ability to not always have to look to him for answers. It also gave us control of the system and our progress by letting us think for ourselves about what was good and bad.

I hope our readers have brought this same generosity of heart and willingness to explore to this work.

Wing Chun Family Tree (abridged)

詠春拳術源流表
(約表)

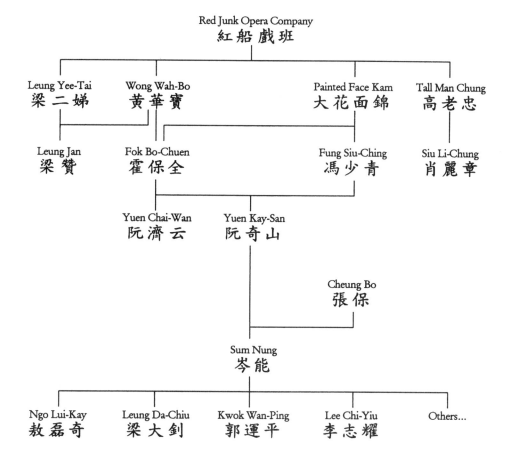

Red Junk Opera Company
紅船戲班

Leung Yee-Tai
梁二娣

Wong Wah-Bo
黃華寶

Painted Face Kam
大花面錦

Tall Man Chung
高老忠

Leung Jan
梁贊

Fok Bo-Chuen
霍保全

Fung Siu-Ching
馮少青

Siu Li-Chung
肖麗章

Yuen Chai-Wan
阮濟云

Yuen Kay-San
阮奇山

Cheung Bo
張保

Sum Nung
岑能

Ngo Lui-Kay
敖磊奇

Leung Da-Chiu
梁大釗

Kwok Wan-Ping
郭運平

Lee Chi-Yiu
李志耀

Others...

Glossary

Terminology is often neglected when a martial art is transmitted in a language other than that in which it was originally conceived. Although practice is important, understanding must also follow. Over the generations, practitioners have helped pass along their own understandings and insights through the terminology they used while teaching the art.

In an attempt to be both thorough and precise, the first section of this glossary provides the traditional Chinese characters and pinyin romanizations for the names and terms used herein. Entries are alphabetized according to their romanized Cantonese spelling. Names of places remain romanized in Mandarin pinyin. Other popular rendering will be noted where appropriate.

The second section provides a Cantonese/English and English/Cantonese reference for the terminology.

A deep language, Chinese words often represent several different ideas. Although an attempt has been made to utilize translations that capture the essence of the terms but it is beyond the scope of this volume to fully explore each and every word. Those who wish to gain a more complete understanding are encouraged to further investigate the Chinese language.

Names

區仕	Au Si (Ou Shi)
區瑞枝	Au Soi-Jee (Ou Ruizhi)
八合會館	Baat Hop Wui Goon (Ba He Hui Guan)
白鶴寺	Bak Hok Jee (Bai He Si)
白鶴拳	Bak hok kuen (bai he quan)
白眉派	Bak Mei pai (Bai Mei pai)
陳華順	Chan Wah-Shun (Chen Huashun)
鄭康銓	Cheng Hung-Chuen (Zheng)
(張)阿七	(Cheung) Ah Chut (A Qi)
張保	Cheung Bo (Zhang Bao)
張五	Cheung Ng (Zhang Wu)
周國泰	Chow Gwok-Tai (Zhou Guotai)
朱壽禮	Chu Sau-Lei (Zhu Shouli)
大花面錦	Dai Fa Min Kam (Da Hua Mian Jin)
大力姚才	Dai Lik Yiu Chui (Da Li Yao Cai)
豆皮濟	Dao Pai Chai (Dou Pi Ji)
董全錦	Dong Chuen-Kam (Dong Quanjin)
董植	Dong Jik (Dong Zhi)
峨嵋山	Emeishan (O Mei San)
霍保全	Fok Bo-Chuen (Huo Baoquan)
佛山	Foshan (Fat San)
福建	Fujian (Fukien)
馮少青	Fung Siu-Ching (Feng Shaoqing)
馮挺	Fung Ting (Feng Ting)
高佬忠	Go Lo Chung (Gao Lao Zhong)

廣東　Guangdong (Kwang Tung)
廣西　Guangxi (Kwangsi)
廣州　Guangzhou (Kwang Chow, Canton)
鶴山　Heshan (Hok San)
香港　Hong Kong (Xianggang)
湖南　Hunan
紅花會館　Hung Fa Wui Goon (Hong Hua Hui Guan)
洪家拳　Hung ga kuen (Hong jia quan)
紅門會　Hung Mun Wui (Hong Men Hui)
紅船戲班　Hung Suen Hay Ban (Hong Chuan Xi Ban)
至善禪師　Jee Shim Sim Si (Zhi Shan Chanshi)
江西　Jiangxi (Kiangsi)
趙簡卿　Jiu Gan-Heung (Zhao Jianqing)
關椿元　Kwan Jong-Yuen (Guan Zhuangyuan)
郝寶全　Kwok Bo-Chuen (Huo Baoquan)
郭富　Kwok Fu (Guo Fu)
郭俊芬　Kwok Jin-Fen (Guo Junfen)
郭運平　Kwok Wan-Ping (Guo Yunping)
黎仰翹　Lai Yeung-Yin (Li Yangqiao)
劉老威　Lao Lo-Wai (Liu Lao Wei)
李志耀　Lee Chi-Yiu (Li Zhiyao)
李俊明　Lee Chung-Ming (Li Zhongming)
李廣海　Lee Gwong-Hoi (Li Guanghei)
李文茂　Lee Man-Mao (Li Wenmao)
梁博鎏　Leung Bok-Lao (Liang Boliu)
梁大釗　Leung Dai-Chiu (Leung Dazhou)
梁贊　Leung Jan (Liang Zan)
梁恩　Leung Yan (Liang En)
梁二娣　Leung Yee-Tai (Liang Erdi)
梁陰堂　Leung Yum-Tong (Liang Yintang)
盧建雄　Lo Kuen-Hung (Lu Jianhong)
呂四娘　Lui Sei-Leung (Lü Siniang)
龍形拳　Lung Ying kuen (long xing quan)
馬仲如　Ma Jung-Yiu (Ma Zhongru)
盲威　Mang Wai (Mang)
苗順　Miu Shun (Miao Shun)
吳仲素　Ng Jung-So (Wu Zhongsu)
五枚師太　Ng Mui Si Tai (Wu Mei Shi Tai)
敖磊奇　Ngo Lui-Kay (Ao Leiqi)
彭就　Pan Chao (Peng Jiu)
蛇形拳　Sae ying kuen (she xing quan)
小少佳　Siu Siu Gai (Xiao Shao Jia)
順德　Shunde (Shun Dak)
四川　Sichuan (Szechuan)
肖麗章　Siu Li-Chung (Xiao Lizhang)
少林寺　Siu Lam Jee (Shaolin Si)
岑芝　Sum Jee (Cen Zhi)
岑能　Sum Nung (Cen Neng)

新錦	Sun Kam (Xin Jin)
摔跤	Sut gow (shuai jiao)
太極拳	Tai gik kuen (tai ji quan)
譚向明	Tam Heung-Ming (Tan Xiangming)
攤手五	Tan Sao Ng (Tan Shou Wu)
螳螂拳	Tong long kuen (tang lang quan)
天地會	Tien Dei Wui (Tian Di Hui)
鐵臂能	Tiet Bei Nung (Tie Bi Neng)
謝頌飛	Tse Chong-Fei (Xie Songfei)
韋玉生	Wai Yuk-Sang (Wei Yusheng)
永春拳	Weng chun kuen (Yong Chun quan)
詠春拳	Wing Chun kuen (Yong Chun quan)
黃貞	Wong Jing (Huang Zhen)
黃華寶	Wong Wah-Bo (Huang Huabao)
二公	Yee Gung (Yan Gong)
嚴詠春	Yim Wing-Chun (Yan Yongchun)
嚴二	Yim Yee (Yan Er)
嚴四	Yim Sei (Yan Si)
嚴三娘	Yim Sum-Leung (Yan Sanliang)
葉準	Yip Chun (Ye Zhun)
葉問	Yip Man (Ye Wen)
葉名深	Yip Man-Sun (Ye Mingshen)
于樂剛	Yiu Lok-Gong (Yu Legang)
阮濟云	Yuen Chai-Wan (Ruan Jiyun)
阮祖棠	Yuen Jo-Tong (Ruan Zhutang)
阮寵明	Yuen Chong-Ming (Ruan Chongming)
阮奇山	Yuen Kay-San (Ruan Qishan)
阮老楂	Yuen Lo Jia (Ruan Lao Zha)
肇慶	Zhaoqing (Siu Hing)

Terminology

擺樁	Bai jong (bai zhuang)
白鶴擒狐	Bak hok kum wu (bai he qin hu)
北拳	Bak kuen (Bai quan)
鏢指	Biu jee (biao zhi)
膀手	Bong sao (bang shou)
半攤膀	Boon tan bong (ban tan bang)
鏈橋	Chan kiu (chan qiao)
鏈紙皮	Chan jee pai (chan zhi)
撐掌	Chang jeung (cheng zhang)
黐手	Chi sao (chi shou)
沉肘救手	Chum jaan gao sao (chen zhou jiu shou)
沉橋	Chum kiu (chen qiao)
衝錘	Chung choi (chong chui)
打包肘	Da bao jaan (da bao zhou)
打沙包	Da sa bao (sha bao)
打手頸	Da sao geng (da shou jing)
打洋燭	Da yeung juk (da yang)

底掌	Dai jeung (dizhang)
搭橋	Dap kiu (da qiao)
頂掌	Ding jeung (dingzhang)
獨龍錘	Duk lung choi (dulongchui)
奪命刀	Dit ming do (duo ming dao)
筷子功	Fai jee gung (kuai zi gong)
反擒拿	Fan kum na (fan qin na)
飛鏢	Fei biu (fei biao)
伏手	Fook sao (fu shou)
虎尾腳	Fu mei gerk (hu wei jiao)
耕手	Gaun sao (geng shou)
耕手	Gaun sao gwa choi (geng shou gua chui)
掛錘	Gwa choi (gua chui)
跪地偏錘	Gwai dei pien choi (gui di pian chui)
跪地偏馬	Gwai dei pien ma (gui di pian ma)
跪馬	Gwai ma (gui ma)
跪馬錘	Gwai ma choi (gui ma chui)
角馬	Gwok ma (jiao ma)
氣功	Hei gung (qi gong)
起膝	Hei sup (qi xi)
開式	Hoi sik (kai shi)
空椿	Hong jong (kong zhuang)
圈手	Huen sao (juan shou)
子午錘	Jee ng choi (zi wu chui)
楂拳	Jia kuen (zha quan)
箭錘	Jin choi (jian chui)
箭馬	Jin ma (jian ma)
扣搭手	Kao dap sao (kou da shou)
扣攋手	Kao lop sao (kou lie shou)
扣手	Kao sao (kou shou)
拳法	Kuen faat (quan fa)
擒拿	Kum na (qin na)
功夫	Kung fu (gong fu)
拉腰	Lai yiu (la yao)
欄手	Lan sao (lan shou)
欄手衝錘	Lan sao chung choi (lan shou chong chui)
練功	Lien gung (liang gong)
練功式	Lien gung sik (liang gong shi)
連環錘	Lien wan choi (lian huan chui)
里簾陰陽掌	Loi lim yum yeung jeung (li lian yin yang zhang)
落肘	Lok jaan (luo zhou)
攋手	Lop sao (lie shou)
六點半棍	Luk dim boon gwun (liu dian ban gun)
碌手	Luk sao (lu shou)
埋肘	Mai jaan (mai zhou)
武術	Mo sut (wu shu)
木人椿	Muk yan jong (mu ren zhuang)
黏單橋	Na dan kiu (nian dan qiao)

南拳	Nam kuen (Nan quan)
外搭	Ngoi dap (wai da)
外家	Ngoi ga (wai jia)
外攔	Ngoi lop (wai lie)
外鐮手	Ngoi lim sao (wai lian shou)
內搭	Noi dap (nei da)
內家	Noi ga (nei jia)
內攔	Noi lop (nei lie)
內鐮手	Noi lim sao (nei lian shou)
按手	On sao (an shou)
批肘	Pai jaan (pi zhou)
拍手	Pak sao (pai shou)
抛膀	Pao bong (pao bang)
偏錘	Pien choi (pian chui)
偏馬	Pien ma (pian ma)
偏身錘	Pien san choi (pian shen ma)
偏身馬	Pien san ma (pian shen ma)
破掌	Po jeung sao (po zhang)
破中手	Po jung sao (po chong shou)
扑翼掌	Pok yik jeung (pu yi zhang)
殺橋	Saat kiu (sha qiao)
蛇形手	Sae ying sao (she xing shou)
三拜佛	Sam bai fut (san bei fo)
三品掌	Sam pan jeung (san pin zhang)
三星錘	Sam sing choi (san xing chui)
散手	San sao (san shou)
收拳	Sao kuen (sou quan)
收式	Sao sik (sou shi)
雙圈手	Seung huen sao (shuang juan shou)
小練頭	Siu lien tao (xiao lian tou)
腎氣歸元	Sun hei gwai yuen (shen qi gui yuan)
十字手	Sup jee sao (shizishou)
十二式	Sup yee sik (shiershi)
十二散手	Sup yee san sao (shi er sanshou)
藤圈	Tan huen (teng juan)
攤手	Tan sao (tan shou)
推掌	Toi jeung (tui zhang)
吞手	Tun sao (tun shou)
蝴蝶掌	Wu dip jeung (hu die zhang)
護手	Wu sao (hu sao)
日字衝錘	Yat jee chung choi (ri zi chong chui)
二字箝羊馬	Yee jee kim yeung ma (er zi qian yang ma)
二字箝陽馬	Yee jee kim yeung ma (er zi qian yang ma)
二字雙刀	Yee jee seung do (er zi shuang dao)
移馬	Yee ma (yi ma)

Bai jong	assume post
Bak hok kum wu	white crane seizes the fox
Bak kuen	Northern boxing
Biu jee	darting fingers
Bong sao	wing arm
Boon tan bong	half-dispersing-half-wing
Chan kiu	shovel bridge
Chan jee pai	paper shoveling
Chang jeung	supporting palm
Chi sao	sticking arms
Chum jaan gao sao	sinking elbow saving arm
Chum kiu	sinking bridge
Chung choi	thrusting punch
Da bao jaan	wrapping hitting elbow
Da sa bao	Sand bag hitting
Da sao geng	striking wrist
Da yeung juk	candle hitting
Dai jeung	low palm
Dap kiu	joining bridge
Ding jeung	butting palms
Duk lung choi	single dragon punch
Dit ming do	life-taking knives
Fai jee gung	chopstick work
Fan kum na	counter seizing & holding
Fei biu	flying darts
Fook sao	controlling arm
Fu mei gerk	tiger tail kick
Gaun sao	cultivating hand
Gaun sao gua choi	cultivating hand hanging punch
Gua choi	hanging punch
Gwai dei pien choi	kneeling side punch
Gwai dei pien ma	kneeling side horse
Gwai ma	kneeling horse
Gwai ma choi	kneeling horse punch
Gwok ma	angle horse
Hei gung	breath/intrinsic energy work
Hei sup	rising knee
Hoi sik	opening form
Hong jong	air dummy
Huen sao	circling arms
Jee ng choi	meridian punch
Jia kuen	closing fist
Jin choi	arrow punch
Jin ma	arrow horse
Kao dap sao	detaining joining arm
Kao lop sao	detaining grasping arm
Kao sao	detaining arm
Kuen faat	boxing methods

Kum na	seizing & holding
Kung fu	effort
Lai yiu	pulling waist
Lan sao	barring arm
Lan sao chung choi	barring arm thrusting punch
Lien gung	training work
Lien gung sik	training work forms
Lien wan choi	linked chain punch
Loi lim yum yeung jeung	inside outside yin & yang palms
Lok jaan	dropping elbow
Lop sao	grasping arm
Luk dim boon gwun	six-and-a-half-point pole
Luk sao	rolling arms
Mai jaan	closed elbows
Mo sut	martial arts
Muk yan jong	wooden dummy
Na dan kiu	sticking single bridge
Nam kuen	Southern boxing
Ngoi dap	outside join
Ngoi ga	outside family
Ngoi lop	outside grasp
Ngoi lim sao	outside sickle hand
Noi dap	inside join
Noi ga	inside family
Noi lop	inside grasp
Noi lim sao	inside sickle hand
On sao	pinning hand
Pai jaan	hacking elbows
Pak sao	slapping hand
Pao bong	throwing wing
Pien choi	side punch
Pien ma	side horse
Pien san choi	side body punch
Pien san ma	side body horse
Po jeung sao	cleaving palm
Po jung sao	center cleaving arm
Pok yik jeung	flapping wing palms
Suut kiu	killing bridge
Sae ying sao	snake form hand
Sam bai fut	three prayers to Buddha
Sam pan jeung	triangle palms
Sam sing choi	three star punch
San sao	separate hands
Sao kuen	ending fist
Sao sik	closing form
Seung huen sao	double circling arms
Siu lien tao	little first training
Sun hei gwai yuen	kidney breathing invigoration

Sup jee sao	cross shaped arm
Sup yee sik	twelve forms
Sup yee san sao	twelve separate hands
Tan huen	rattan ring
Tan sao	dispersing arm
Toi jeung	pushing palm
Tun sao	swallowing arm
Wu dip jeung	butterfly palms
Wu sao	guarding arm
Yat jee chung choi	vertical shaped thrusting punch
Yee jee kim yeung ma	trapezoid shaped clamping goat horse
Yee jee kim yeung ma	trapezoid shaped clamping groin horse
Yee jee seung do	parallel shaped double knives
Yee ma	moving horse

English/Cantonese

Air dummy	*hong jong*
Angle horse	*gwok ma*
Arrow horse	*jin ma*
Arrow punch	*jin choi*
Assume post	*bai jong*
Barring arm	*lan sao*
barring arm thrusting punch	*lan sao chung choi*
Boxing methods	*kuen faat*
Breathing work	*hei gung*
Butterfly palms	*wu dip jeung*
Butting palms	*ding jeung*
Center cleaving arm	*po jung sao*
Candle hitting	*da yeung juk*
Chopstick work	*fai jee gung*
Circling arms	*huen sao*
Cleaving palm	*po jeung sao*
Closed elbows	*mai jaan*
Closing fist	*jia kuen*
Closing form	*sao sik*
Controlling arm	*fook sao*
Counter seizing & holding	*fan kum na*
Cross shaped arm	*sup jee sao*
Cultivating hand	*gaun sao*
Cultivating hand hanging punch	*gaun sao gua choi*
Darting fingers	*biu jee*
Detaining arm	*kao sao*
Detaining grasping arm	*kao dap sao*
Detaining joining arm	*kao lop sao*
Dispersing arm	*tan sao*
Double circling arms	*seung huen sao*
Dropping elbow	*lok jaan*
Effort	*kung fu*

Ending fist	*sao kuen*
Flapping wing palms	*pok yik jeung*
Flying darts	*fei biu*
Grasping arm	*lop sao*
Guarding arm	*wu sao*
Hacking elbow	*pai jaan*
Half-dispersing-half-wing	*boon tan bong*
Hanging punch	*gwa choi*
Inside family	*noi ga*
Inside grasp	*noi lop*
Inside join	*noi dap*
Inside outside yin & yang palms	*loi lim yum yeung jeung*
Inside sickle hand	*noi lim sao*
Joining bridge	*dap kiu*
Killing bridge	*saat kiu*
Kidney breathing invigoration	*sun hei gwai yuen*
Kneeling horse	*gwai ma*
Kneeling horse punch	*gwai ma choi*
Kneeling side horse	*gwai dei pien ma*
Kneeling side punch	*gwai dei pien choi*
Life-taking knives	*dit ming do*
Linked chain punch	*lien wan choi*
Little first training	*siu lien tao*
Low palm	*dai jeung*
Martial arts	*mo sut*
Meridian punch	*jee ng choi*
Moving horse	*yee ma*
Northern boxing	*bak kuen*
Opening form	*hoi sik*
Outside family	*ngoi ga*
Outside grasp	*ngoi lop*
Outside join	*ngoi dap*
Outside sickle hand	*ngoi lim sao*
Paper shoveling	*chan jee pai*
Parallel shaped double knives	*yee jee seung do*
Pinning hand	*on sao*
Pulling waist	*lai yiu*
Pushing palm	*toi jeung*
Rattan ring	*tan huen*
Rising knee	*hei sup*
Rolling arms	*luk sao*
Sand bag hitting	*da sa bao*
Seizing & holding	*kum na*
Separate hands	*san sao*
Shovel bridge	*chan kiu*
Side body horse	*pien san ma*
Side body punch	*pien san choi*
Side horse	*pien ma*

Side punch	*pien choi*
Single dragon punch	*duk lung choi*
Sinking bridge	*chum kiu*
Sinking elbow saving arm	*chum jaan gao sao*
Six-and-a-half-point pole	*luk dim boon gwun*
Slapping hand	*pak sao*
Snake form hand	*sae ying sao*
Southern boxing	*Nam kuen*
Sticking arms	*chi sao*
Sticking single bridge	*na dan kiu*
Striking wrist	*da sao geng*
Supporting palm	*chang jeung*
Swallowing arm	*tun sao*
Three prayers to Buddha	*sam bai fut*
Throwing wing	*pao bong*
Thrusting punch	*chung choi*
Tiger tail kick	*fu mei gerk*
Training work	*lien gung*
Training work forms	*lien gung sik*
Three star punch	*sam sing choi*
Trapezoid shaped clamping goat horse	*yee jee kim yeung ma*
trapezoid shaped clamping groin horse	*yee jee kim yeung ma*
Triangle palms	*sam pan jeung*
Twelve forms	*sup yee sik*
Twelve separate hands	*sup yee san sao*
Vertical shaped thrusting punch	*yat jee chung choi*
White crane seizes the fox	*bak hok kum wu*
Wing arm	*bong sao*
Wooden dummy	*muk yan jong*
Wrapping hitting elbow	*da bao jaan*

Rene Ritchie has been studying the Yuen Kay-San system of wing chun kuen under the guidance of Ngo Lui-Kay since 1990. He is co-author of the book *Complete Wing Chun: The Definitive Guide to the History and Traditions of Wing Chun Kung-Fu* and has written articles for *Martial Arts Masters, Inside Kung-Fu* and *Martial Arts Illustrated* magazines and the *Wing Chun Kuen Today* newsletter (www.wing-chun-today.com). He has created and maintains the www.wingchunkuen.com site on the Internet World Wide Web and is currently working on several forthcoming projects. Rene works and practices in Eastern Canada.